(My Wife Told Me)

Make This World
a
Better Place
for our
Grandchildren

(My Wife Told Me)

Make This World a Better Place

for our Grandchildren

Tobias Jungreis

ThomasMore®
– An RCL Company –
Allen, Texas

Send all inquiries to:

THOMAS MORE PUBLISHING
200 East Bethany Drive
Allen, Texas 75002-3804

Telephone: 800-264-0368 / 972-390-6300

Fax: 800-688-8356 / 972-390-6560

E-mail: **cservice@rcl-enterprises.com**

Website: **www.ThomasMore.com**

Printed in the United States of America

Library of Congress Catalog Number: 2001 134093

7478   ISBN 0-88347-478-6

1 2 3 4 5   05 04 03 02 01

·⊷ DEDICATION ⊷·

TO MY INCREDIBLE and edible grandchildren whose future lives will, hopefully, be more pleasurable and peaceful as a result of our efforts to make this world a better place.

   This book could not have been written without the encouragement, giggling, and professional editing of my wife, Shirley.

Tobias Jungreis

❖ Contents ❖

Introduction

WHAT AWAITS my rapidly growing grandchildren in the world in which we live? Moral decay, an increasing number of alternate life styles, war, threats of war, growing welfare rolls, a widening drug culture, and the expanding grip of crime on our lives.

What can I, an aging, selfish, naughty, crotchety guy with a twinkle in my eye, do to stem the tide and reverse the sinking ship of human behavior that underlies this sometimes ugly morass?

At my wife's beckoning (and dare), I have tried to break down all of the above mess into daily situations of human beings dealing with fellow human beings. If, with all my devilishly wrong instincts, I can turn my life around and become a generous, considerate, gentle person, I believe everyone can.

(My Wife Told Me) Make This World a Better Place for Our Grandchildren reviews common, everyday situations, such as what to do when receiving someone else's mail, giving directions to a stranger, dealing with someone talking too loud in a movie theater. Most books available today either confirm how rotten we are, how beyond repair, or, conversely, that "I come first." Neither mindset encourages forward progress. *(My Wife Told Me) Make This World a Better Place for Our Grandchildren* encourages understanding, patience, generosity, friendliness, rethinking the situation, and the desire to do better. Only through these little steps in the right direction can we rise to the level that we were truly created to achieve, and make this world a better place.

· 1 ·

Humor is the
Lubricant of Life

WE GET A FLAT TIRE mid-span on a narrow one-lane bridge. Our backhand winning shot at match point sails wide, opening the door to you know what. The zipper on our fly is jammed in the open position as we step to the lectern for a rare televised appearance. We finally enter the stock market and it turns out to be the day it begins its historic decline. We split the seam of our tuxedo pants as we are getting out of the car at a very important family wedding.

Our best day of business potential is ruined by lousy weather. Our cakes sometimes decide not to rise. The best fish we ever caught is lost as we raise it from the water into the boat. Our weekly lottery numbers will probably never come in (unless we accidentally forget to buy a ticket one week). We get stuck on a malfunctioning elevator for two hours on the way to game seven of the World Series. We see our child lose out in the casting for the lead role in the school play. We experience a "bad hair day" just before a long-awaited first date. We find that our beloved pet cat has disappeared one day, never to be seen again.

We can expect to suffer illness and pain. We are all destined to lose loved ones. We are all destined to die.

How do we deal with all this mess?

More than lots of money, more than strong egos, more than infinite patience, more than individuals who we hope will protect us, we need a sense of humor if we want to make this world better. If we are lucky, we are born with one. If we are not so blessed, we must develop one. Humor enables us to deal with a horrible situation, a setback, disappointment, or loss. It is a necessary diversion. It is a deflection of the pain, a distraction.

Rather than dwelling on the obvious catastrophe and its miserable consequences at hand, we need to see the silly or ironic side of the moment. The glass becomes half-full rather than half-empty. For example, you're getting pulled over by a state trooper for speeding. As you are slowing down to the side of the road with the big blinking red light behind you, you can perhaps chuckle at the thought of the approximate number of times you have sped *without* getting caught. This would reduce the fifty-dollar fine on average to about thirteen cents for each time you weren't caught. Or you could consider the fifty dollars your annual contribution to the Policemen's Benevolent Association. And when they come around collecting at holiday time, you can securely say that you gave already. Or, you can wonder (it better be silently) if they take Visa at the courthouse, because you are relentlessly accumulating mileage toward an important plane trip.

Or, you can ponder what great excuse you might give the trooper to see if you can talk your way out of a ticket. Maybe you are an obstetrician racing to a hospital to deliver a baby. (You'd better not be wearing a bathing suit and baseball cap). Or maybe you left a cake in the oven and if you don't get back quickly, your oven will burn down a ten-story building. Or maybe somebody is locked in a meat freezer and you are speeding desperately to let him out. Anyway, as you accept your ticket, you thank the policeman for his watchful care of the highway and tell him that his conscientiousness is making the driving experience more secure and safe for everyone.

Humor is infectious. In the hospital lounge near the room of the terminally ill relative you are visiting, silliness and laughter *is* appropriate. In order to liven up the unfortunate patient, you have to bring lightness and joy into the room. The patient doesn't want to recount how many needles he's experienced in the last twenty-four hours. He wants some levity. He wants to hear who's doing what to whom in the world outside. Or who is not doing what to whom. It is an incredible joy to say something ridiculous to a patient hooked up to a half-dozen tubes, and see a grin break out on his or her face. It is like melting a glacier. That smile had not been used for such a long time that it was almost forgotten.

Humor can be uplifting and certainly distracting, but it must also be used with great care. My wife and I once visited our daughter-in-law who was in the hospital after giving birth to her first child, my second granddaughter. With my son and the new baby present, we were all having a pleasant conversation, discussing, among other things, who this cute little half-day-old baby looked like. At one point, I asked to hold the baby, and enjoyed this precious little miracle. Alas, my poor daughter-in-law was uncomfortable with her cramping and fatigue, so I looked for a way of distracting her. I focused on the name band on the tiny arm of this little being that I was holding and, across the room, I asked the new mother, "Who is Gonzales?" (You know from the cover of this book that their name was certainly not Gonzales?) "What?!" shouted my stunned daughter-in-law, involuntarily jumping ten feet in the air and momentarily forgetting her cramping. "Just kidding," I sheepishly said, immediately regretting having startled this new mother at a very emotional time. "I apologize." Yes, humor must be used with great care.

Humor is also a means of breaking up the seriousness of a conversation—when the debaters are getting hot and heavy discussing politics or religion or government spending or gun control or the safety of our drinking water. I, who seldom discuss politics, enjoy the verbal battles sometimes going on around me. I really do a lot of learning just by listening about subjects that have no great interest to me. I am more apt to be daydreaming about the next day on my sailboat or my most recent incredible racquetball victory, or my next hot bath, or the ultimate, my next bagel and marmalade and coffee snack.

In summary, our apparently normal, tension-filled, complicated world is a hodge-podge of screw-ups, misunderstandings, ironies, coincidences, and oxymorons. If we can laugh at the latter and laugh at ourselves and not take all apparent truths too seriously, we can slither safely through the daily minefield that we call life.

2

Pun . . . ishment

RECENTLY, a few of my contemporaries were debating the past and current nationalities of the popes. Why were they mostly from this country, sometimes from that country, *never* from that country? This led to the subject of the poor health of the current pope (John Paul II) and who were the likely successors. Now I know this subject *is* of utmost importance to many people and *is* really of consequence to the world at large. Why, though, for the life of me, is this of any concern to six people riding in a car on a gorgeous summer day on a country road with a fantastic view of a picturesque wooded mountain range? I could not resist. "From my reading, (that will be the day!) it looks like the heir apparent to the current pope is a Cardinal Secola from Pittsburgh." "Really?" they chimed in, "we never heard of him." "Well, I do know one thing, " I continued, "When he *does* become pope, he'll be known as Pope Secola (say it quickly!).

At this point, my alleged buddies knew they had been had, that I knew nothing about the papacy, and that my addition to the conversation was really a monkey wrench to bring them back to focus on the beauty of the day.

Puns are said to be the lowest form of humor by the critics. But they are really a lot of fun to think up, especially while waiting at red lights. Puns are a mind game. They don't add anything of substance to the world. They are brain teasers. They are like the mental games of anagrams, Scrabble® or Boggle®. The English language is so complex and full of words that sound alike or are spelled alike that toying with the written word has infinite possibilities.

Where do you go with puns? They are not ordinarily jokes told at a party to make people laugh. Well, for the editor of a major newspaper or magazine, they can be used as an eye-catching title for a story or a light filler between articles. And, if you are talented enough to make up your own and have plenty of time on your hands, and have plenty of postage stamp money around, you can submit them to magazines for income. (Do not, I repeat, do *not* give up your day job).

The real product of producing puns is the private chuckle, which, like an after-dinner mint or a hot bath, makes your day a happier, more relaxed one. It eases the tension of the moment and squeezes out a smile on your face. Two puns I remember reading in a magazine many, many years ago have never left my head. They made such an impression on me. "Speeding at 70 miles an hour, the car approached the coroner." The other was the text of a postcard written by a traveling salesman on a business trip to Florida to his wife: "Dear Marcia, the trip so far is going wonderfully. I'm having a great time. The weather is glorious. Wish you were her."

A few originals that I have sold, but certainly could be thought up by anyone, are:

"Definition of hair transplant: Reseeding for the receding."

"Definition of perjury: Truth decay."

"New Laundromat in town: The Clothes Spin."

"Name of a piano-organ store: Precious Tones."

"A recent survey showed that 62% of wealthy male retirees invest in municipal blondes."

"Bear in mind, most people prefer not to go camping."

3

A Piece of Cake

I WAS BLESSED with a father who saw life from a humorous perspective. He was indeed the first Good Humor man. He instilled in me a distorted way of looking at things. Also, in terms of life's setbacks, he categorized two types: those that *you* create, deliberately or accidentally, and those that are *acts of God*. The former unpleasantnessses are harder to deal with because you yourself make them happen. The latter problems are more easily blamed on some outer force—God, the weather, the lousy ways they make tires these days, the lousy ways they make everything nowadays, etc.

Entering a popular bakery some time ago in a relative hurry (I'm always in a hurry), I took a number from the number machine and got in line. Looking around, I saw that there were about twenty-five people ahead of me. I considered getting back in my car and returning an hour later. However, it was raining, there were no other bake shops around, the store was due to close in about half-an-hour, and my mission and purchase was critically important for an upcoming celebration.

Once you realize that you are stuck in a situation that you have no control over, it is very soothing to your system to take note of what's nonsensical about bakery behavior. First of all, the salespeople behind the counter are always, by definition, eighty years old, or older. They don't hear so well. They don't move so fast. They all seem to add up your bill with a little broken pencil stub on a crinkly piece of paper they pull out of their pockets. And, yes, they don't add so fast.

"How much sheet cake do you want? Two pounds? Well, my last piece is two and a quarter pounds. Do you want the whole piece? Where are you? Sadie, what happened to my customer? Where did she disappear to? Oh, there you are, Mrs. Martin. Do you want the whole piece?"

And, of course, there is always the *pièce de résistance*, the box fastened with string, a custom carried on since George Washington's days. The cord for the cake box comes from above and must be wound around the box three times in each direction and must be cut by winding it around one's hand and snapping. The dexterity to do this does not come so easily to senior citizen salesladies, and very predictably causes the line to slow down even more.

To make the time pass and ease the waiting (which seems even longer than the wait in a physician's waiting room, where you at least have some outdated magazines to flip through), you ponder some cute audible monologues, some passive and some more aggressive. If you feel somewhat relaxed, you can just start mumbling about the baby you left in the middle of your double bed, certain that this stop at the bakery would just consume three or four minutes.

As you gradually raise the volume of your voice, you calculate that it is improbable that the granddaughter you are watching has the motor skills to turn over enough times to reach the edge of the bed. And, after all, if by some improbable freakish chance, the baby does roll off the edge, the rubberized padding of the carpet ought to be sufficient to at least partially cushion the impact of her landing. Then again, you say softly, your daughter is still mad at you since the baby fell off the bed only ten days earlier while in your care. "But," you ramble, "there is no reason to rush these hard-working bakery employees just because I miscalculated the timing. I'll just deal with the anxiety, and my daughter's anger and the potential of serious injury without burdening anyone else. There *is*, after all, only a forty percent chance, really, of serious injury." . . .

If you feel terribly brave, you can cheer yourself up by imagining yourself to be a sanitary inspector bursting through the bakery door. What will you say? Well, in the meanest voice you can fashion, you announce that you are an inspector from the municipal health department and have been sent here to check out a series of complaints. Flashing an imaginary badge, you loudly demand the list requested for analysis by your superior at the laboratory—five eclairs, three challahs, a pound and a half of plain sponge cake, and seven apple turnovers (which just happens to be the list given to you by your wife)—all to be tested for E. coli, Salmonella, and "mad cow disease." "And," you declare with a dramatic sweep of your arm, "if there is any delay whatsoever in getting these samples, I have the authority to shut this store down right here and now!" So much for humoring yourself, but it does use up a few minutes and now there are only eighteen people ahead of you.

Another mischievous dally I have toyed with is to buy a set of numbers from a stationery store, to be used at moments like this. Most take-a-number machines dispense somewhat similar tickets. The next time I might be sent on an errand to this infamously crowded bake shop, I would be prepared. After entering, I would take a number and lose myself in the crowd for a few minutes. "Number seventy-four" is called out. The real number seventy-four and I would both hand our numbers simultaneously to the waiting salesperson. If she complains that there can't be two "number seventy-four" tickets, you impatiently advise her to get her broken number machine fixed. Of course, you are both waited on, and you are out of that disaster area in minutes.

But, remember, to truly make this world a better place, these plots remain in the realm of mental gymnastics as your place in line advances and you engage a few of your fellow customers in pleasant conversation.

4

"Thanks" Is a Sound, Not a Feeling

PICTURE A WORLD in which everyone says "Thanks" for every gesture of kindness or assistance someone has given to them. There would be a groundswell of warmth arising among people. Mankind, created to be sometimes cruel, possessive, and aggressive, would transform into a gentle and kinder version. People would feel good about each other—less competitive, less suspicious and less hostile.

To be thanked makes us feel good. It means we made someone happy. It means that we are *capable* of making someone else happy, which is a feeling not universally felt by all individuals. Giving always benefits the donor more than the recipient. (Unless someone, for some reason, decides to leave me a million dollars in his will, I guarantee that I will experience more joy than he.) Many of us who are not so secure in terms of self-esteem or self-worth or self-confidence often neglect the one behavior that powerfully reverses these self-doubts. This is the act of giving to another. There is no more humanizing gesture available to us in so many forms than the act of giving— whether it be a little kindness between human beings or an institutionalized giving like charity work or volunteer work.

Sometimes our giving is formally thanked, whether it be a recipient's "Thank you" or a charity organization's receipt. Sometimes we "experience" the thanks. We might see a "smile of gratitude" or an expression of relief or merely observe others "doing better" as result of our kindness. Rabbi Moses Ben Maimon described four forms of giving, starting with the lowest form:

1. The donor and the recipient know each other,
2. the donor knows the recipient while the recipient does not know the donor,
3. the donor does not know the recipient but the recipient does know the donor,
4. neither the donor nor the recipient know one another.

Sometimes the thanks is merely a silent wave of the hand or, in the case of your pet dog, a wagging tail. Sometimes it's a maitre-d's wink after you slip a ten-spot into his palm, or the first mate of a fishing boat saluting after you have tipped him for cleaning some fish.

The best acknowledgment of appreciation, the one which reinforces the act of giving most positively is the *audible* "Thank you." It leaves no room for doubt. It is the strongest form of thanks because it requires one to *say* something. That sound is more powerful than a facial expression or a gesture or an indirect indication of appreciation.

The heard "Thank you" induces the same reaction as a flower being watered and fertilized. The flower stands tall and invigorated. We humans respond the same way.

On a given day, the opportunities to say "Thank you" come up dozens of times (unless you are a night watchman all night and sleep all day). The list is endless:

- To the person who enters your office building and holds the door open for you.
- To the waitress who brings you your morning coffee.

- To the mailman who drops off your mail (and if you're lucky, mails the letters you are sending out that you leave for him in your door slot.)
- To the bus driver who picks up your precious children and takes them to school.
- To the sanitation man, emptying your garbage pails, that you pass as you head for your car in the morning.
- To the supermarket cashier who checks out and bags your groceries.
- To the dry cleaner attendant where you rushed to drop off your dress shirts.
- To your neighbor for dropping off your mail that accidentally went to him by mistake. (No. You do not stop saying "thanks" to your mailman, as a result.)
- To your daughter who found your glasses, which you misplaced. (You need glasses to find your glasses.)
- To the driver who lets you take that hard-to-find parking spot who responded to that look on your face that said, "Please, I saw that spot first and, besides, I am desperately late."
- To the bank teller who stopped her coffee break to take care of your deposit because she knows you as a regular customer.
- To your customers who support your business. You are thanking them for choosing you, acknowledging that they have the choice to patronize one of your competitors.
- To the telephone operator who puts through your urgent call.

The list goes on. The above dozen are just for starters. They could all take place the first two hours you are awake in the morning. You have the rest of the day to flood the world further with your reservoir of good feeling.

⁙ 5 ⁙

Cursing Is People Pollution

HAVE YOU EVER swum out to a raft at a public lake where several teens were sunning themselves and chatting away? "Oh f . . . , I forgot my f . . . keys in my f . . . jacket. Now, how the f . . . am I to get into my f . . . house?" Answer: "Well, just f . . . the f . . . keys. you can f . . . sleep in my f . . . house tonight." Sad to say, this is our practiced language today. If you don't hear it during the summer at a lake, try sitting unnoticed in the back of a school bus. You'll hear the same.

For umpteen years, our movies were way behind the times. The characters on the screen spoke polite, proper, grammatically correct language while the customers in the theater were cussing away at the refreshment stand. Sadly, our movies and TV programs have finally caught up, with some films' ratings now being lowered for severely vile language alone.

There was a time when if a child cursed publicly, it was an immediate reflection on his parents. For sure, he learned his bad words from the adults in his house. Not so today! We have broadened our use of expletives to the point where they have become the norm. Curses are learned in school, at camp, on TV—everywhere. When nudity, even fleeting, first appeared in the movies, it not only got a special rating code, but it was noted by and discussed by the movie reviewers as a highlight (or lowlight) of the film. In time, nudity has come to receive only a ho-hum mention in the review summary, in small print. So, too, with cursing and profanity. It is here with us—even in our dictionaries.

What a great sadness! I miss the loftiness of the spoken language. There was a straightforwardness and purity of expression. To make a point or to express extreme emotion, adjectives and adverbs were used, not expletives. The old system works. We did effectively understand each other without the smut.

It is time in our new century to do better. Cursing is a pollution of our souls no different than emissions polluting our lungs. Its practice lowers our level of humanity, notch by notch, in terms of loftiness. We ought to fight it like we fight other forms of pollution—by voluntary controls, by education and, if necessary, by regulation. Churches and synagogues can preach and give classes on appropriate language in the same way they guide us on morality and business ethics. The movie industry can set up guidelines for acceptable language and, hopefully, use a voluntary code system as it does for nudity and violence. School principals can set up educational programming on unacceptable language just as they set aside time for workshops on drugs, alcohol and smoking. All of these voluntary efforts can be backed up with stricter regulation as needed.

We adults must show the way in the privacy of our homes. Profanity, or its acceptance, starts within our families. Conversely, its unacceptability also begins in the home. We have to be the role models for the next generation. There is nothing sadder than to have one of our children or grandchildren arrive home from the school bus and utter a curse word totally out of context. Not only did this pure tot hear a bad word, but he remembered it enough to repeat it, to be "one of the guys."

Better speech does make better people. Better people make a better world.

⋯ **6** ⋯

Let's Abbreviate the use of Abbreviations

DRIVING ALONG the LIE, wearing my BVD's, I saw an apparent UFO while sipping my MBT. TGIF!

For the results of the MRI of my ACL, 1 was told to send a SASE, ASAP.

We live in a strange world. The dodo bird, the Studebaker and the eight-track tape have become extinct, but the use of abbreviations has increased in alarming proportions.

When a group of people are sitting in a social setting, and one person is chattering away, chances are that he will use abbreviations as a matter of course. Some of those listening will know exactly what he is talking about. Some won't recognize the abbreviations, but will, somehow, take an educated guess from the context of what he is saying and be able to keep up with his line of thought. Some, however, will not recognize his "code letters" and be lost from the rest of the conversation.

Abbreviations are overused. If their purpose is literally to save time, it just takes one listener to say, "What's a PSA?" This query and the response to the query uses up more time than the milliseconds originally saved.

Is their purpose to upgrade the spoken language so that a group of letters, well recognized, becomes a new individual word, like IOU or UCLA or CD? Thus, the speaker is making a statement that saying CD rather than certificate of deposit is upgrading the English language! He perceives that the abbreviated form shows a more cultured and educated use of conversation! Well, the speaker is taking a risk that the abbreviation he is using is a step forward rather than a step backward as far as the language is concerned.

There is also the risk that the abbreviation has more than one meaning. Is someone handing over money to the IRA representative supporting a revolutionary organization, the Irish Republican Army, or is he making an individual retirement account annual contribution to his bank representative. Is someone giving a present of a CD (certificate of deposit) to his grandchild putting money away toward his college education or adding a compact disc to his music collection?

The worst possibility is that the use of the abbreviation is signaling that he, the speaker, is a member of a special club, one of the chosen few who know what the letters stand for. This is most annoyingly used by members of a particular profession or business. "Oh, we'll check his PCV" (packed cell volume). Or "We'll just hire an R & B (rhythm and blues) group." Or "It will probably read over twelve PPM" (parts per million). This is all well and good if a bunch of physicians or restaurant owners or toxicologists are talking shop together. However, as soon as they are joined by the rest of the world population, or sometimes just their wives, the wording used should be universally understood for courtesy if not communication purposes.

Which reminds me of the story of the group of elderly ladies from New York, touring the state of Texas, whose tour bus was passing one vast cattle farm after another one afternoon. They made a stop at a particular beef cattle farm. One senior lady, wandering around, chanced upon the farm manager. She said, "Boy, I am really impressed by the enormity of the acreage here. Where I come from, the farms are tiny by comparison. Sir, what is the name of your farm?"

"He responded, "It's the 4BQQQFRVVA Hereford Beef Farm."

To which she said, "Wow! That is really a very impressive name. You must have thousands of heads of cattle on your farm."

He answered, "Well, not really, ma'am, not too many survive the branding!"

Well, I'm off to send in my RSVP (*Respondez, s'il vous plait*).

7

Talking in Motel Halls

TALKING IN THE HALLS of a motel or a hotel is a small infraction that can have a huge impact on our fellow human beings. We should really strive to do better. It's funny. In our rooms, we never raise our voices. We keep the TV volume level low lest the sound carry through the walls and disturb our neighbor. We have a sense of partnership with the many people in separate cubicles sharing one building, and our instincts are basically correct. If we find something in our rooms, left behind by a previous guest and overlooked by the chambermaid, we don't hesitate. We take it right down to the front desk and we are confident we are bringing relief to someone.

Oddly, it is in the halls that we are guilty of gross obliviousness. There are some people who cannot fall back asleep once they are awakened. Yet, when we leave our motel rooms, we slam our heavy doors as though no one were nearby, when in reality, most of the rooms might well be full. There are some guests who work most or all of the night and sleep during the day. Yet when we approach or leave our rooms, we talk and laugh loudly in the halls, unaware of our rudeness. When we are in our rooms at a resort or an inn, when our doors are shut, we are within our own private worlds. We read, sleep, cuddle, and ponder privately. Outside noise breaks the spell. It intrudes on our perceived insulation. It undoes the lovely view out the window.

This humorously reminds me of my bad luck at certain high-class corporate resort centers. The luxury heaped upon the guests is quickly apparent when you first enter your room—refrigerator, stocked bar, in-room coffee, all sorts of toiletry giveaways.

(I always wondered if the delightful little wicker baskets that the shampoos and lotion bottles come in are mine to keep as well. I love those baskets, but I resist taking them. I always picture the ultimate embarrassment. Being surrounded by security officers, friends, family and other guests in the busy lobby in front of the check-out counter. I am forced to open my sloppily packed, full suitcase and dump all the contents onto the lobby floor until they finally get to the object of my petty larceny—the little wicker basket. Warned that I was "this close" to being handcuffed and arrested, I am allowed to leave in shame, in public view, with a promise that I will never grace these doors again.)

So there you are in your Waldorf-like palace of a room. What you failed to realize signing in is that just next door to your room is the large maintenance room. This room is on every floor. It stocks towels, fresh sheets and pillowcases, paper supplies, etc. Most important, it is where all the morning chambermaids meet with their supervisors—at 7:00 A.M., no less—to be assigned their duties. Checkout time might be 11:00 A.M. or noon, but this crew starts its work very early, beginning with the rooms just vacated, as early as 7:00 A.M. What seems like an enormous union meeting takes place just outside your door and lasts an hour, nonstop, in different languages. They have a lot to go over—who goes where, who cleans what, who is sick and didn't show, what was on TV last night (they spend most of this meeting hour giggling), and what movies they saw. I, who had a late dinner and watched a late TV movie, paying for the privilege, had been hoping to snooze deliciously until at least 9:30 A.M. But no! The troops assemble outside my door almost every time. I seem to attract them like honey attracts bees!

On the other side of my famous door, I can hear the 7:05 A.M. vacuuming going on in the room next door where the guests checked out early. The crew of two are having a wonderful time energetically cleaning. I hear them moving furniture. I hear them giggling. They vacuum endlessly. Of course, in order to talk to each other, they must shout above the vacuum noise. Help! I'm exhausted. I'm overpaying for my room and my comfort, but I feel I'm in the middle of a big parade. I don't understand. If checkout time is 11:00 A.M. and check-in time is 3:00 P.M., doesn't that leave an ample chunk of time for the ground crew to do their thing? Aren't the managers aware? Why the gangbusters at 7:00 A.M.? And it's a no-win situation to complain about it when I check out. If they just say, "I'm sorry. We'll look into it," it doesn't return my missed sleep. Yet, on the other hand, their offense isn't "heavy" enough to ask for any kind of compensation. *C'est la vie.*

So, fellow sore losers who love to stop at inns and motels on your vacation sorties and romantic getaways, keep this in mind when you check in. Always request a room far from laundry rooms, supply closets, stairs (beware the echo), elevators (how can you resist chit-chat while waiting), ice machines, vending machines, and employee union offices. And when you are up early or in the halls, this is your turn to be gracious with your fellow human beings, to speak softly and tread lightly. It will contribute toward a better world.

·· 8 ··

Returning Phone Calls

YEARS AGO, when you wanted to make a long-distance phone call, you had to ask for the assistance of an operator. You could not do it by yourself. You dialed the operator and gave the distant phone number to her. (There were no "hims.") She connected you. My father, while a very humorous man, was sometimes short on patience. He was an all-world practitioner of the art of sarcasm. He would dial an operator and if the phone rang more than two times, when she did finally pick up, he would calmly say, "Operator, did I wake you?"

Phone service has come a long way. Years ago, there were no area codes. A second line was rare. If a physician headed the household, the family members had to end their personal calls after three minutes to keep the phone free for Dad's practice.

Today, the reverse is true. Phone paraphernalia is increasing almost exponentially. It is routine *not* to answer phones but rather to monitor them as they come in, and pick and choose which calls to answer. We are protected by our answering machines. We can electronically obtain the phone number of someone who is dialing us as well as prevent someone we dial from getting our number. We can see people we are talking to on a screen. Via the computer, we can automatically contact a thousand customers with a business message without ever talking into a mouthpiece.

Our society needs a major improvement and that is in returning phone calls. I am not referring to calls pitching you to switch phone companies. Nor do I have a problem disregarding unsolicited sales calls, especially those timed during the supper hour. I am addressing ordinary phone calls made to you by human beings, friends or acquaintances, or someone referred to you by someone else you know. There are those individuals who simply do not call back. The obvious questions are: "How do they live with themselves?" and "What do they say when they meet someone by chance who has phoned them numerous times without a response?" It is an odd discourtesy. It is as though someone were looking you in the eye, asking you something, and you do not respond. It's like someone greeting you while you just stare or look away.

Why do non-phone-call-returners not return calls? There are many possibilities:

1. They are "on overload," too busy, and they figure that if the caller wants them enough, they will certainly call again.
2. They don't like the caller or the message or the question the caller has for them, so why respond? This would include callers to whom they owe money, callers asking for charitable contributions, those people who irritate them for some reason, or those people with whom they prefer to discourage the continuation of the relationship.
3. Their mother-in-law called—(just kidding).
4. They assume the attitude of a casting director who has the power to pick and choose when and if and to whom to respond.

I would like to submit that if our world is to be upgraded in terms of human relations, phone call messages should be returned when reasonably possible. Anger and frustration would be diminished. Communication, whether it be positive or negative, is always good. It clears the air. The worst villain deserves this minimal courtesy. In responding, we learn the difficult skill of the clarifying dialogue. We can deal with an annoying salesperson directly and briefly without the need to hang up on them or to curse them out.

(When my daughter was in college, she did part-time telephone solicitation for a charitable organization for a little income. She described the great range of responses she got to her disruptive phone calls. For her, the few pleasant people more than made up for the rude majority. This experience, to this day, has made me a notch more gentle and patient with the unsolicited solicitors who interrupt my routine.)

You really never know when you get a message from a relative or an acquaintance how urgently your response is needed. Many callers are reluctant to be specific when leaving voice mail. It may be a cry for help. It may be a need to cry on someone's shoulder. It may be for help with a decision. It may be a request for professional advice, whether it be for a sick child or a bland salad. The quicker you return the phone call, the more apt your response is to be timely and helpful.

Don't try to get away with, "I tried to reach you several times" because many of us have machines that document every call. Don't say "I tried but your number was busy" because many have "call waiting" or "overflow numbers."

Respond, sooner or later, but respond. It is no different than saying "Please" or "Thank you" or holding the door open for someone. It gives us all a better feeling about our fellow human beings, and certainly contributes toward making this world a better place to live.

❖ 9 ❖

Sorry, Wrong Number

"HELLO, can I speak to Harry?"
"Who?"
"Harry."
"No Harry here."
Click.

"Hello, can I speak to Harry?"
"Who?"
"Harry".
"Wrong number."
Click.

"Hello, can I speak to Harry?"
"Who?"
"Harry."
"Wrong number."
"Wait! Harry told me his number was 343-2110."
"No."
Click.

"Hello, can I speak to Harry?"

"Who?"

"Harry."

"Wrong number."

"Wait! Is there no Harry at 343-2110 or did I dial wrong?"

"You dialed 2210."

"Well, thank you very much."

Click.

Wouldn't it be great if a wrong number or a wrongly dialed number were answered patiently and courteously?

Wouldn't it be great if the response weren't with an annoyed tone and the cutoff clicker were slower on the trigger?

Isn't this a possible opportunity for helping our fellow human being?

True, this intrusion may have come at a critical time—in the middle of supper, in the middle of a serious conversation or on the final play in the football playoff game. It may have followed two crank calls or a bunch of telephone solicitations. However, we must think of this caller as we would someone we don't know calling up for help. Somehow, over time, wrong numbers have gotten a bum rap. It is time to change this and show much needed compassion. Consider the wrong number as a bonus opportunity to encourage someone with a little cheer.

·· 10 ··

Public Phone Booths

PUBLIC PHONE BOOTHS are a dream come true, if you have ever traveled around the world. They are the common person's answer to the cellular phone generation. They provide a sense of humility to those using them—unlike the impression one gets, for example, from the deeply tanned driver of a Mercedes convertible holding the wheel with one hand and chatting on his cell phone with the other as he speeds along (with a beautiful blond companion in the next seat, of course). You can dial anywhere with a credit card. If you have no money and no credit card, you can call the operator and speak to a live person just for the asking. You can make a long distance call without a credit card, providing you are the type of person who walks around with a full roll of quarters in your pocket. You can call someone collect.

If you are lucky, there may even be a shredded yellow pages directory under the telephone that's less than ten years old. If you are lucky, the public phone booth won't be next to a loud noise source like a tavern juke box, where you can talk but you can't hear. If you are lucky, the phone won't be in a public place like the entrance into the restroom in case you have to make a sensitive call and need a little privacy.

If you are lucky, you will not select one of those pay phones that cuts you off if you don't come up with the overtime money within two seconds. This always seems to happen to me at the pay phone at the airport when I arrive late at night on my way home after a lengthy trip, with all my baggage, exhausted. When I finally get through to the private cab company and am trying to get out the words to describe the precise spot where the driver should pick me up, "big brother" with or without the two-second warning, cuts me off. I am now giving the baggage area number to a dial tone. If I'm staring at all the coins I'm holding in the palm of my hand, I doubt that I have the hand-eye coordination to get the proper coins into that ever-so-skinny slot in two seconds, anyway. Especially if it's cold and I'm shivering and I'm miserable and tired and unhappy that I had to leave my sunny paradise!

If you are lucky, you might even be surprised to find some change in the return coin slot. In trying to raise the ethical level of life, I find it best to pocket this money rapidly and not think too much. Because if you do, you end up in deep trouble. After all, it truly belongs to someone else. It could belong to an unfortunate foreign visitor who thinks that what goes into the phone is gone forever because in his country there are no return slots. It could belong to a poor elderly soul who just forgot to look for his refund. It could belong to a struggling local phone company that just canceled its annual dividend to thousands of stockholders.

But other than taking the money, what are you really supposed to do? Leave it there and hope the next person using the phone is a stockholder of said dying phone company and getting what is truly coming to him? You are a good person. Take the money and rationalize that the last ten times you dialed the wrong number, you were too sloppy and lazy to call for a refund.

If you are lucky and have a good back, you might find some change scattered on the floor of the phone booth—probably by someone wealthy who couldn't care less, or someone with too sore a back to bend down.

There are certain rules of etiquette about the use of public phones that would give all of us a better feeling about each other and make this a better place for our grandchildren. This is not just a casual request for courtesy, because very often the use of a pay phone is accompanied by great anxiety and tension. Someone must be reached quickly, often immediately, to prevent a health problem, to solve a monetary situation, or to prevent a scheduling mix-up.

First, if someone is waiting to use the phone, and no other phone is visible nearby, our conversation should be ended as soon as our reason for calling is completed. We have no idea of the extent of the urgency of the next person in line. I have seen long lines at the only phone at a tennis match or in the theater or at a catering hall. I am saddened when the one on the phone is leaning against the wall, giggling, relaxed, just chatting away, while those in line, dependent on the caller's integrity, are going through a slow burn (or a real panic).

When there is a waiting line, or even only one person waiting, it is not the time for a social call, nor the occasion to review all the movies we have seen recently. And if we are on the phone and this call has to be lengthy for business reasons or whatever, tell the one waiting for you, "I'm sorry, but it looks like I'll need at least ten minutes." Or reassure them, "I need just one more minute." This brief communication is very important. It's also friendly, considerate and compassionate. When there is just one phone, all of us waiting become partners in a little life drama, and our humanity is on the line. We must strive to be more aware.

Conversely, do not crowd the one on the phone to the point where there is no privacy. Create a decent distance as you would waiting in line at a cash machine. He or she might be proposing marriage (probably she). He or she might be timing contractions to a physician (probably she). He or she might be selling out his whole stock portfolio based on a quarter of a point change (probably he). He or she might be begging his or her marriage partner for forgiveness (probably he). He or she might be God unrecognized (probably she). Anyway, don't try to read lips (you probably can't do it unnoticed any way). Don't laugh at something the caller says (you're too obvious). Don't say "God bless you" if he or she sneezes (unless it's a cute she). And, finally, don't start inching closer to the booth unless the conversation goes on more than two minutes. (That's more than enough time to propose, sell your equity holdings, or even for God to elucidate a commandment).

It's just a phone booth. It's just a situation of more than one person needing the same item. Nothing earth shattering here. It happens every day, over and over. But it's a wonderful opportunity to make human beings really feel good about one another, which always makes this world a better place.

⁓ 11 ⁓

Getting Someone Else's Mail

SO WHAT SHALL I DO? I got someone else's mail. Well, isn't it obvious? I give it to the postman and say it's not mine. But this simple solution is easier said than done. There are endless problems. Granted, there is nothing monumental at stake, that is, unless it's *your* important letter that went to the wrong place. Here are some typical problems or things to think about:

1. You don't recognize the name of the addressee or the address so you cannot simply take the letter to the neighbor next door.
2. You get the letter on Saturday and if your intention is to give it to the postman, you don't know where to put the letter for two days and how to get yourself to remember on Monday that you have the misdirected letter in the first place.
3. You are never home during the day so you don't even know who your postman is or what time he delivers. So how do you get the letter to him?
4. It looks like junk mail, like one of the telephone long distance companies' special offer to dislodge you from the one you have, and you are tempted to risk going to jail by tossing the letter into the garbage.

5. You don't know if you should scrawl something on the letter, like "Moved" or "Addressee Unknown" or "Doesn't Live Here" or "Right Address, Wrong Party" or just one big messy smudge with a magic marker through the name and address. (I'm sure a quick call to the post office would obtain the correct procedure.)

6. Maybe it's best to toss all letters that aren't yours into a utility basket in your garage and try to remember to take any accumulated batch to the post office the next time you have to go there. Then, again, maybe your garage is so cluttered that you would have trouble remembering which of a dozen baskets you set aside for what purpose.

7. Maybe I don't go through my own mail for several days. Is the possibility of having someone else's letter in my house or office going to force me, by guilt alone, to look through my mail daily?

8. Suppose I repeatedly get the mail of someone on my block with a similar name and despite all my appeals to him to change something or use an initial instead of our common name, he does nothing. Is some kind of revengeful action or merely an annoying action permissible here?

9. Suppose I get someone else's free sample of shampoo or soap or calendar, and I like that sample and I want it? Isn't there a Latin saying someplace that amounts to "All's fair in love and mail?" Isn't possession three quarters of the law of ownership? Aren't samples nonreturnable? Are you allowed to keep the sample and return the address card to the postman?

The direction of all these conjectures is kind of obvious—to make every effort to get that mail back to its rightful owner. How willing am

I to extend myself and make an effort for my fellow human being—especially in a situation like this where he is totally unaware that he is dependent on my good instincts? He has no clue, so I am really on my own and unobserved in this testing of my character. Although the percentage of meaningful mail received today, much of it churned out by a computer, is tiny, there is always that chance that this misplaced letter has some meaning far beyond that which we can fathom.

So I will pray to the Almighty for still another degree of patience and goodness of heart to make it easier for me to do the right thing. And while I'm praying, I'll also pray that He (or is it She?) give that same additional degree of patience and goodness to all the neighbors on my block. After all, as it is for many other people, the arrival of my daily mail brings with it the potential of excitement, wealth, fame, or the answer to my prayers.

⚊ 12 ⚊

Giving Directions

THERE IS A STORY as old as the hills that tells of a lady tourist who approaches a dignified looking man on a New York City street and asks him how long it will take to walk to the Empire State Building. The man looks at her but doesn't answer. She repeats her question. Again, he is attentive but fails to respond. With impatience and annoyance, the woman walks away and down the street, apparently to seek out someone else for help. The man now calls out to her, "It will take about 15 minutes." She stops short, runs back to him and asks, "Why didn't you answer me in the first place?" With a gentle smile, he responds, "Don't you see, ma'am, I had to see how fast you walk!" Corny, but classic.

I read someplace that a study was made in several metropolitan areas. The result was that two out of three people approached for directions by a stranger gave an inaccurate answer. This seemed odd to me when I first heard of it until the day that *I* gave directions in *my own* neighborhood, and realized later that they were unclear, and rather misleading. Contrary to the wise-guy advice of never getting instructions from a woman, the wrong advice can come from anyone, man or woman or undecided.

So, as we try to improve the quality of relating to our fellow human beings, and at the same time try to raise ourselves to a higher level (boy, I need all the help I can get!), here is an easy area. Giving wrong directions can delay the victim by a few minutes from his destination or worse. He can miss a train or his return ride back to who knows where. I remember traveling out west with my wife by car. One incorrect turn cost us ninety miles out of the way! That ain't chopped liver.

When someone approaches us for directions, or asks by phone for the best route to get to our home, we should think of this as a special opportunity for assistance. It's no different than lending money or guiding a blind person across a heavily trafficked street. The recipient is totally dependent on our integrity, as well as our accuracy. Can a right turn be misconstrued? ("Well, I guess the road angles to the right and it's actually not really a turn.") Does route 78 "become" route 22 or is route 22 an exit off route 78? Is there an ongoing construction detour on a road that you forgot to reveal? Is a particular landmark that is critically essential clearly visible from *this* direction, or in the dark? ("Y'know, you're right. I forgot they close early on Thursdays and shut their lights off.")

On directions involving several legs of a journey, it is imperative to give the approximate time or mileage on each leg so that a traveler will sense if he's been driving too long and stop for help. A comedian once described the difference between directions given in the New York City area versus the rest of the country. In New York, "How far is it to Manhattan?" will always produce an answer in an amount of time, like "About twenty minutes."

Or "How far is it to the Whitestone Bridge?"

"Oh, about an hour."

The rest of the country answers in miles! "How long a drive is it to the post office?"

"Two and a half miles."

New Yorkers actually do not know (and are not interested) in the actual distance. It makes no difference! A one-mile trip can take twenty minutes if there is always heavy traffic on a particular road.

Giving directions is a special opportunity for us to shine, and let us be thankful for the opportunity. Actually, just today I was at the receiving end of the following interchange. Paying my bill at the exit booth of a municipal parking lot in Poughkeepsie, New York, this morning, (Do you think I spend the whole day writing?) I asked the cashier for the quickest way to get onto Route 55 East. She said, "It's easy. Make a left at the stop sign and then another left at the next stop sign. At the traffic light, make a right and you'll see the sign." Well, needless to say, it never happened. There were four turns, with stop signs, before I even got out of the parking lot. There were no traffic signals in sight, and I spent the next twenty minutes reluctantly taking the scenic route home through the historic section of Poughkeepsie.

Which reminds me of the story of the drunkard who walks up to a bartender and slurs, "How do I get to the men's room?" The bartender tells him to go down the corridor and then make a left, then a right and then a left. The inebriated man proceeds to make a right and a left and a right, walks into an open elevator shaft and falls one floor to the bottom. Lying on his back, dazed, he makes out several figures peering down at him from the shaft door a flight above. "Wait," he hoarsely yells, "Don't flush me down!"

Well, you get the point.

13

Crosswalk for All Walks of Life

IN BROOKLINE, Massachusetts, there is a pedestrian crosswalk across busy Harvard Avenue. There is a sign at the curbs at both ends of this specially marked walk. It states that Massachusetts law requires all vehicles to stop if someone is crossing the street at this crosswalk—otherwise, expect prosecution and heavy fines.

In San Antonio, Texas, at a busy corner, there are electric "Walk" and "Don't Walk" signs. When the "Don't Walk" sign is lit, a whole crowd of pedestrians stops and waits for the sign to change even if there are no cars in sight. They follow the lighted directions religiously.

In Manhattan, New York City, the same light "Walk" and "Don't Walk" signs are present in the congested midtown area. These signs are totally disregarded by pedestrians. Their decision to cross or not to cross is based totally on the automobile traffic in front of them. If there is enough time to dart across the street between passing cars, they are off and running. There is no honor system. There is no real system. The "Walk" and "Don't Walk" signs are only used by New Yorkers as a glancing indicator if the traffic light is about to change or not.

(There is a story told of a drunken old man holding a cellular phone leaning on a pole at a busy Manhattan corner. He manages to hit the button on his phone which automatically dials his grown daughter. In his slurred speech, he asks her to please pick him up as he is too dizzy to walk any farther. She asks him exactly where he is now. In a daze, he looks up and answers, "I'm at the corner of "Walk" and "Don't Walk.")

In Rego Park, Queens, in New York City, there is a heavy immigrant population especially from the former USSR (Oops! an abbreviation, but an acceptable one, right?) and Czechoslovakia. The area is quite congested with both people and automobiles. The cars characteristically speed, even on the side streets. The pedestrians show their cultural difference. They cross the streets slowly. They do not look both ways first. They step off a curb and never look up! It would appear that they are more worried about tripping over a pebble than they are about being hit by an automobile. They behave, correctly or incorrectly, as though they have an automatic right of way to the point where they don't even bother to look. As you observe them, you just pray that the Lord is on their side. New York, unlike Massachusetts, does *not* have a crosswalk protection mentality.

We have, in addition, individuals with different levels of caution, urgency and courtesy. Some drivers slow down or stop, to let people cross the street or allow drivers to exit from their driveways onto the main thoroughfare. Some drivers, law or no law, traffic light or no traffic light, don't touch their brakes unless they actually see a cop or their fuzz-buster goes off. Some people on foot are so caught up in their thoughts that they are on "automatic" at a crosswalk and never notice red, green, or in-between.

Some walkers are so frightened by car traffic that they will wait and wait in any situation until they feel totally secure about their safety. Some people feel strongly that either automobiles or pedestrians have the right of way, and their behavior reflects that mindset. Some individuals are so respectful of laws and are so confident that they will be universally obeyed that they never double-check a situation for safety sake. Some drivers are pussycats if they are out pleasure driving but are monsters if they are under time pressure. And so on and so forth.

What is at stake with this hodge-podge of custom and regulation? Death, disfigurement, injury, and grieving relatives.

We need a thorough study undertaken of various state and city laws, as well as statistics on pedestrian injury in areas with and without these regulations. To improve this precious world we live in for your grandchildren as well as mine, I think we need a *national* law that is uniform for all. This federal law would be taught to all schoolchildren and to new and old drivers. This one system would become part of our culture. We would not need to worry about a family that relocates from a state with protective crossing laws to one without. We will all do it one way, like one big happy family.

··· 14 ···

Any Room in Your Car?

YOU ARE LEAVING from a wedding or a lecture with a forty-five-minute drive ahead of you. Your car is full. Someone runs over to you as you are getting your coat. "Do you have room for one? Someone needs a ride to your area." This is always a tough call, an uncomfortable one. The fit is already tight. For the sake of one, should you inconvenience others?

I think that if you get into the habit of saying "Yes," this positive effort will ripple off into many other daily situations where people can be helped. Obviously, if there is a danger of driving an overcrowded car or the request is really problematic in some way, you can turn down the plea in good conscience. But, where you can, give the little extra effort that will bring so much joy to the recipient, and a much bigger joy to the donors.

Your table at a wedding is full, people's shoulders and place settings almost touching. "Have you room for two more?" you hear. The answer "Sure" should come from your lips before you even look around. Everyone has to squeeze a little? So what! At most weddings or organizational dinners, people move around a lot. Actually, they may sit only when the food is being served. Most of the time, they are up and around—chatting, dancing, visiting other tables, etc. But you made that quick unconditional gracious welcome. You helped the hostess or dinner chairman seat a couple of displaced persons. These hapless souls—late arrivals, perhaps, adrift without a place setting, without a home, were given comfort by your delightful gesture.

Can you put up some kids staying in your neighborhood over the weekend? "Why, absolutely!" you tell the weekend coordinator. "We've got some extra cots. We'll borrow some mattresses from a neighbor. We'll double up a little. It will be fine."

How rewarding it is for your soul to extend yourself, to welcome a stranger, to crowd yourself a little. Giving is such a joy—to make another human happy and wanted.

Is this world going to be improved so that my grandchildren will have a fulfilled life? You bet it is, if everyone says "Sure!" in every arena where a helping hand is needed.

·· 15 ··

Car Signs

ROAD RAGE is a growing phenomenon around the country. I am certain that it always existed. One day, it just got a catchy title and a little newspaper attention. Loosely defined, it is the violent outcome of a difference of opinion between two people who happen to be in cars, whereby at least one of them goes off the emotional deep end.

Road rage is just one extreme of the continuum in which there is misunderstanding between two drivers. The nature of driving brings out the difference in people. Some are in a hurry, like taxis heading to the airport under tremendous pressure, while others may be taking a casual trip, more focused on listening to taped music than on what time they will arrive. Some individuals are aggressive by nature, trying, often without even realizing it, to out-hustle the competition. Their opposites are casual, avoid confrontation, and allow the aggressor to have his way.

Some people are risk takers, boldly and quickly surmising that their cars can fit through a narrow space, and willing to take the consequences of their unscientific judgment. Their opposites are cautious and calculating, avoiding even the remotest chance of putting a slight nick on their car. Some drivers are angry human beings, life not having been too kind to them, and their interpretation of any questionable car maneuver is a challenge to their ego and manliness. Others simply see driving as just another activity of the day, like doing the laundry or shopping for food, and treat it in a relaxed routine fashion.

So here we have drivers from every type of family background, every economic status, every disposition, every daily schedule, every driving skill, in autos in a great variety of repair or disrepair, thrown into close partnership because they, by chance, happen to be driving on the same road together at the same time.

What is the most significant and unique aspect about drivers' behavior to one another that differs from all other human exchange?

The answer is the lack of opportunity for communication between those in cars.

They are enclosed, usually behind closed, even tinted, windows. Cars move at different speeds in different lanes, so that lining up to pantomime a message, due to factors out of your control, is at best difficult. Especially during rush hour, if one were to slow down to signal a nearby driver to pull his car abreast, he would be honked to death by oblivious drivers whose only concern is to keep moving.

It is exactly this inability to have thirty seconds worth of communication that leads to misunderstandings, outbursts of emotion, anger, and occasional violence. If only someone behind a wheel who cuts off his neighboring auto could basically explain the circumstances contributing to why he did what he did or merely say, "I'm sorry." Communication, difficult at best even with people who know each other, is notably absent here, in situations where it is desperately needed.

Which comes to my invention. Every new car made should be equipped with a long narrow retractable billboard on top that is capable of flashing momentarily lit messages in full sentences. The messages would turn off after a few seconds so as not to be too distracting to nearby drivers. The messages must be clear and concise. They can be activated with a console under the dashboard to the right of the driver. There can be a beginner "package" of ten messages to handle the most frequent situations, or a fifty-pack for those as much interested in communication as they are in getting someplace, or who like to socialize once behind the wheel. My invention will be called the "CHATTER BOX."

What might be the ten most frequent messages? (This might be as difficult to decide as which are the seven wonders of the world, or the best ten movies of the last century.)

1. *Possible beginner set:*

I'm sorry	Your tire looks low
Thank you	Your door is open
I didn't mean to do it	Your trunk is open
I can't make out what you're saying	Your right/left brake light is out
I need directions	You are dripping gas.

2. *A friskier set of ten to be imagined, but not really used:*

You're cute	My other car is a Jaguar
Same to you, brother	Pull over so we can talk
Get a real car	Your car needs washing
Careful! I can read lips!	We're senior citizens; forgive us
You can pass now	What's the hurry?

Seriously, though, only the first ten are necessary. And of the first ten, the first is the most important. Apologizing and the ability to say, "I'm sorry" will diffuse ninety-five percent of road rage. The "Chatter Box" will calm any misread communication or action. It will open up a dialog to stymied, frustrated individuals.

··· 16 ···

Rubbernecking Is
a Pain in the Neck

I WOULD LIKE to rid this world of rubbernecking, not only for the sake of my wife and my grandchildren, but for all of us. "Rubbernecking," loosely defined, is the deliberate slowing down by drivers in order to get a longer look at something happening on the side of the road—either side of the road. It is very widespread, as you know, especially if you live in or around a big city and listen to the traffic helicopters during the morning and evening rush hours.

What makes us all slow down when we see the flashing light of a police car or a tow truck or an ambulance, or when we notice two cars just sitting on the shoulder of the road?

Secondly, why do we slow down ten days in a row because of activity off the road? Why don't we become immune? We certainly have no trouble immunizing ourselves to approaching panhandlers, or homeless people curled up in cartons on the sidewalk. Is it the fascination with other people's problems? Is it the magnetism of potential gore? Is it just a source of entertainment during a tedious car ride no better or no worse than glancing at a billboard advertisement? Or, digging a little deeper, does slowing down indicate our rejoicing that misfortune has hit someone else, while we're safe, unhurt.

Be that as it may, it is human nature to be attracted to injury, crime, and violence. This is what sells the most movie theater tickets. This is what keeps us glued to the evening news—the more blood, the higher the ratings. When you think about it, what subjects fill up our news hours? There is always an ongoing criminal trial. There is an earthquake in Africa, a volcano in South America. A fishing boat sinks, killing four sailors. A teenager is stabbed in a fracas following a basketball game. Radioactive leakage is found in the waters surrounding a nuclear power station. Thirty thousand customers have no electricity following a severe ice storm. The airline pilots are on strike following a union dispute stranding thousands of holiday travelers. We keep watching. And after a break for a couple of commercials, we are ready for more. Thirteen champion horses are killed in a stable fire in Kentucky. A cable car carrying skiers up a mountain is hit by a low-flying airplane killing six people. Seventy-two senior citizens are hospitalized after a case of food poisoning at the annual senior center picnic. We never hear enough of it.

So, how can you blame rubberneckers? We have this built-in appetite for gore. Interestingly, however, we do have a limit—not in the quantity of disasters, but rather in the degree of damage that we actually see with our eyes. During the news programs, the news station keeps us in the comfort zone. We see the mildly injured, not the dead. We see aerial shots of fires, not burnt flesh. We see the police rope around the crime scene, not the bodies. The same is true with rubbernecking. We want to see, but we don't want to see too much. We strain our necks, but not too far. We want to get close to the accident, but not to the seriously injured victims.

The bottom line of rubbernecking is that it's a pain in the neck for everyone. It is an abuse of time. It is an inconvenience that we impose on our fellow drivers who cannot pass us while we collectively block the road. And it can contribute to the problem. When we slow down, everyone slows down. Is there a simple remedy? Maybe there is.

When the first police cars arrive at the site of a crash or a disabled car, they should, as they currently do, check out that everyone is all right. Then, what if they set up canvas screens with aluminum frames, ready and rolled up in their squad cars, to block the view of oncoming drivers? It would take three or four screens and a matter of minutes, and the problem situation is removed from sight. Then they set up flares or red cones to keep cars passing smoothly. The far side of the problem scene would stay open to receive service or rescue vehicles. But, as a driver approaching the scene, I only see a canvas wall. I can't see anything behind it. So, while my first instinct is to slow down, I keep going.

Will it work? In time, I think it will. Haven't we accepted canvas partitions to create cubicle workspaces instead of offices? It will become as normal as a nurse pulling a drape around a patient in a hospital bed for privacy. It will feel as normal as a screen in front of a new exhibit being constructed in a museum gallery or a new store in a mall.

Setting up canvas screens has many benefits. It will save countless man-hours for commuters (like me!) who are so frequently forced to arrive late to work. It will give a little dignity and privacy to people unfortunate enough to have been involved in a crash or breakdown. (Not to mention, that it will add jobs to those in the canvas and aluminum pole business.) It will make it easier for safety and rescue personnel to reach the scene, which is of the utmost importance—they won't be held up waiting for rubberneckers to get out of the way!

17

Holding the Door

THIS SIMPLE ACT of kindness is an instant of compassion that can come up frequently in a given day. It is a marvelous, inexpensive, quick, noncommittal, instantly rewarding, safe, legal, nonpolluting, nonfattening opportunity for doing something for a fellow human being. For those who spend most of their lives not getting thanked enough or ever, here is your chance. It reminds me of the "all-stop" intersections in some big cities. Four drivers pull up to stop signs. All four courteously view each other, and wait. Then, one at a time, one pulls forward, waves "Thanks" to the others and goes on his way. This is repeated as the second driver proceeds from the intersection, then the next, then the next. Mathematically speaking, four vehicles at such an intersection provide for three individuals to give "thanks" and six "thanks" to be received. (Figure it out.)

Since human beings and their actions and responses are unpredictable, many questions go through my head when I attempt to hold a door open for someone as I go in or out of a door:

1. What if the recipient of my generous act doesn't quickly follow me as I hold the door open either because they are older or just slow? This always seems to come up when I am in a hurry. Am I obliged to wait once I commit myself and we make eye contact, or is there a statute of limitations, like two seconds or ten seconds or even thirty seconds?

2. What if the person behind me is more than several feet behind as they follow me? Is there a "distance" statute of limitations? Or am I expected to push the door open and just wait even if

the recipient of my gesture is some distance back? Since I am a walking reservoir of guilt in these person-to-person interactions, as well as having terrific peripheral vision, I deal with this question in perhaps not the nicest fashion. If I sense that my follower is far enough back that waiting for him would delay my forward progress too significantly, I merely push my door forward forcefully, without looking back, and stride right through—as though I were unaware that someone was behind me. This feigned unawareness, besides depriving me of being an instant good person, usually makes me annoyed with myself to the point where it wasn't worth the time saved.

3. Is it required by the second individual to acknowledge the gallant act?

4. Must the acknowledgment be audible like "thanks," or is a smile or a wave ample? I remember recently having a door held open for me by a woman. I was oblivious and proceeded forward, only to hear a muttered curse from the lips of the do-gooder. Maybe an audible signal is a good idea.

5. What if you rapidly push through a door, with your head somewhere up in the clouds, and your door swings back and slams into the person behind you? How serious is the crime? How apologetic must you be? Is there a statute of limitations on the time that it is reasonable for you to remain apologetic? In other words, when can you drop it and go about your business?

6. What if the individual following you is a mother or grandmother pushing a stroller with babies? Is this ho-hum business as usual or the equivalent of a state law requiring you to be helpful until the entourage has safely passed through?

Now that our awareness level of door kindness has been raised a notch or two, we can almost look forward to the next chance to create a "thanks" moment for our fellow human beings.

18

To Tip . . .

TIPPING, paying the gratuity, greasing the palm, schmear—whatever you call it, this is the age-old practice of saying thanks monetarily either before or after a service is rendered.

In industry, it is standard to "gift" someone who is in the position of purchasing your product, in order to induce him to give *you* his business rather than someone else. A children's clothing manufacturer will give a gift or some kind of payment to the buyer of the children's department of a clothing store. A sardine manufacturer will routinely pay a supermarket manager to stock his brand of product on the store's shelves. There is a massive lobbying effort that influences our government officials. Legal or illegal, big scale or little scale, it is a fact of life.

It is the tipping practice from one individual to another almost every day, however, that could use a real revamping, if we want to improve the world for the sake of our grandchildren. Many current tipping practices are totally illogical, unfair, arbitrary, and unnecessary. The bottom line is that they tend to leave those of us trying to be better people in a state of guilt and discomfort.

Take dining in a restaurant, for example, where the restaurant pays its waiters a very low salary—an antiquated system that is universally practiced. The bulk of the waiter's income comes from our gratuity, fifteen percent or more. Why? Why not pay them well to start with for running themselves ragged on a busy evening, and, if necessary, increase the price of the food selections to cover the establishment's cost? Why am I, as a diner, paying an employee's wages?

In ninety-nine percent of the cases, the alleged "special service" that I am receiving is the physical transfer of the plate of food prepared by the cook the distance of twenty feet from the cook's counter to my table. Is this really a special service that calls for a special payout by me? How else am I supposed to receive the food? The service actually provided me is having someone else cook my food instead of me. (Ironically, the cook is the only one I don't have to tip). The onus of the transfer of food from the kitchen to the table belongs to the restaurant. Otherwise, I literally cannot eat anything!

Some restaurants automatically add a fixed percentage of the bill to the check, either to make it easier for the customers, or probably, to be sure no one walks out without tipping sufficiently. Why go through these shenanigans? I don't need to know the restaurant owner's finances or troubles. I don't need to know how his help is being paid or the price of his potatoes that week. Let him put on the menu the price of a selection, calculated any way he wants, just like the price of a pair of shoes in a shoe store. The result is that if I choose to order a certain dish, I pay the written price only, with no extras.

The new system that I am trying to establish is to fix the menu price on a particular item so that it includes both the transportation of the food to my table and the removal of any dishes or silverware necessary to make room for my possible next course. Now isn't that easy? Why do I, the customer, have to think so hard? (Let me see, twice the tax. No, no, move the decimal point over one number to get ten percent, then add half of that ten percent, etc.) I'm here to relax, and to be served!

By the way, who ever deemed appropriate that pouring whiskey from a big bottle into a shot glass with a pre-set level warrants a hefty gratuity?

And, in another area, why do we routinely tip taxi drivers? On an average taxi ride, I spend the first ten minutes (in vain) trying to put on my usually inaccessible safety belt. The next five minutes I spend trying to find the driver's exact name and where to call in case of a problem. This information is not so easily obtained given all the notices now posted in the rear of most cabs. The next five to twenty minutes are occupied with my struggle to calculate the fifteen to twenty percent tip of my probable final fare. This is not so easy!

First of all, every block or so, the fare jumps forward. How do I calculate the waiting time at a long red light? And what are those other numbers lit up on the fare box? Is that for my satchel or attaché case? Is there an extra fare added after a certain time in the evening? Alas, my life is also complicated by the fact that a taxi going from the airport to my home crosses from one county to another, with the second county double the rate of the first! And this, unfortunately, is a trip that I have to make frequently.

(We will not address the standard joke of late night TV hosts who describe out of towners' first exposure to New York City. These newcomers are able to experience the fragrance of French cooking, the pungent smell of Moroccan cuisine, the spicy tang of Middle East specialties, and the fishy air of Japanese sushi – a potpourri of international flavors at its best – and all this before they leave the taxi from the airport!)

When, O' heavenly Father, may I relax during a cab ride? As I fumble to undo my jacket and proceed into my pants pocket to get my wallet, I worry about dropping something valuable onto the floor, losing it forever. In summary, I don't need all this! I am making a rational decision to take a taxi. I am choosing not to rent my own car, get picked up at the airport by a friend or relative, or take the airport shuttle. I have opted to pay retail. The driver has not given me any sort of customized or unique service. True, he has gotten me safely to my destination.

True, he has not gotten me there by some circuitous route. True, he has usually been silent or pleasant. Special treatment? No. The world is crying for a *total* cost on his meter box—to make me enjoy my trip better without the haunting worry of possible underpayment.

Again, wouldn't we all be happier not to have to take off our gloves to fill an expectant palm? Wouldn't this be a step forward toward making this world a better place?

⸺ **19** ⸺

... Or Not to Tip!

IT SEEMS that we are expected to tip for a select group of services only. And the list is not necessarily a logical one. As mentioned above, waiter service and taxi service, often unskilled, should be off the list. On the other hand, I am not expected to tip someone who dry-cleans my pair of pants. Why not? This person has to endure a steamy atmosphere, especially during the pressing of the pants. He has to constantly inhale fumes that may be carcinogenic. He has to quietly tolerate complaints about delays, stains, lost tickets, and sometimes damaged or lost apparel. And for this he gets at most a few bucks.

Also illogical is tipping the chambermaid in your motel or hotel room. The service is not personal. It is not skilled. I am already paying a hefty fee for the room (and certainly the loaded bar in the closet). I am already paying tax and often a service charge. What would happen if I failed to tip? Would the chambermaid get annoyed and not make the bed? Would she hide my cuff links in my slippers? The service she supplies is intrinsic to the hotel's service. It is not an option.

How about the baggage handler at an airport? Now, *he* should get tipped. By lifting my suitcases, he is taxing his back. (Isn't it amazing how reliable these husky handlers are? . . . until the day their back starts aching.) In addition, this poor guy's income opportunities today are shrinking, which is the real reason he deserves my gratuity. He has to compete with other legitimate options available to me—rental carts, often free, or simply rolling my luggage on its own wheels!

What about the parking attendant at the public garage where you leave your car to go to work or to the theater? It is standard to tip this man. (Women, for some reason, have not yet infiltrated this industry. Can you picture the guilt of not tipping a woman! You would not only be a cheapskate. You would be a rogue!) These attendants are all probably nice guys working hard to make a living. However, since these are not self-parking garages, I am not allowed to go up the car elevator to get my own vehicle. So, the parking and retrieving of my car is an integral part of the price I am paying and is not a special service rendered to me.

(This reminds me of the comedy routine describing parking attendants. The car is driven at the parking garage for maybe a minute on arrival and another minute at retrieval by the garage employee. During these two minutes, incredibly, every setting on the dashboard is changed. The radio is turned to a heavy metal rock station. The treble and bass knobs are turned too high. The seat is moved all the way back. The air conditioner is on. The fan is on high—the fan? The side view mirrors are adjusted. The steering wheel is tipped back and the directional signal is on—to signal whom? So much frenzy practiced in our cars!)

Humor aside, there are a lot of good people out there who deserve our tips. To avoid confusion and guilt, though, the list should be shorter—and optional. Certain individuals really do service above and beyond the expected. As mentioned above, cooks in a restaurant are a forgotten lot. It is true that they get paid well—many restaurant managers have to tiptoe around them—and often own the whole place. However, when they are making up a special dish with instructions on salt, sugar, or fat content, they are changing their routines. When they have to split hairs between medium grilled steaks, medium rare, medium well, etc., they are aiming to please.

Another group perhaps who deserve a gratuity are the people working on our bodies in some fashion. If a trained barber cuts your hair in the exact way you instruct him, is this considered an extraordinary service? Debatable. Women's hair? Certainly more is at stake here. The skill of the hair stylist factoring in the ongoing dialogue between the customer and the stylist is a much more personalized and precarious scenario. If a barber messes up a man's head, it will grow back and you start all over in three weeks. A woman's feeling about herself often starts with her hair. Her trust and dependence in regard to her hair stylist by far outranks her relationship with her gynecologist.

We generally tip the manicurist and the shoeshine person. Of interest, we tip for the shining of our shoes and boots, an unskilled labor, while we do not tip for a new heel or new soles or stitching on our footwear, all of which require a much more skilled effort. Nor do we generally give a gratuity to the one who dyes a woman's pair of shoes, a very precise procedure, where the exact match of the shoes and a wedding dress leave no room for error.

We do not give a tip, ordinarily, to most lecturers—at our synagogues and churches, at our community centers, at our local bookstores, or at our garden clubs. Oddly enough, we are almost required to tip a tour guide as we get off the tour bus or merely complete a scheduled tour of some kind. While the chatty guide is usually personable and charismatic, as well as knowledgeable, his imparting of information is the tour we are already paying for.

Again, we end up paying part of his wages that ought to be taken care of entirely by his employer. As we descend the bus stairs, the guide's hand has a dual function, to assist us with the long step and to receive our gratuity. After being charmed by this individual throughout the tour, it is a shame to walk away with the usual uncomfortable questions. Did he expect something? Was my tip stupidly excessive or insultingly small? Was I better off not giving anything? Is it demeaning to a grown, intelligent person to be tipped like a taxi driver?

Trying our best to be good people, we must come to certain conclusions on the subject. First and foremost, we cannot, as individuals, change a currently accepted area of expected tipping unilaterally. This would be clearly rude and insulting. Logical or illogical, in certain scenarios, the "tippee" counts on the money automatically as part of his income. He didn't set up the system.

What to do to effectuate change so that our grandchildren don't have to go through this? The ideal might be an international conference on tipping where heads of government and industry would discuss this subject just as naturally as they discuss other subjects— import taxes, quotas, trade unions, protectionism, tariffs, etc. This not being too feasible, maybe instead a groundswell educational movement could induce the leaders of our service industries to gradually eliminate tipping. All it really takes is a big "NO TIPPING" sign and a raise in salaries to create instant change.

⸳⸳ 20 ⸳⸳

Improving the World of Smoking

FORTUNATELY, I AM a nonsmoker. I've never taken a puff in my life. I was an anti-smoking activist well ahead of my time. Smoke bothered me especially when I was eating and, since my intolerance wasn't widespread at the time, I felt like an oddball and kept my mouth shut. To witness today's universal exposé and crackdown on the tobacco industry is an absolute miracle in my lifetime. It is the experience of seeing a quirky private hate of mine suddenly shared by the entire world, now on my side to eliminate the irritant.

It is certainly well documented today by research studies that smoking causes so much disease and sadness, with monumental associated costs, that our lives on this earth would be wonderfully enriched by the phasing out of legal smoking, however long it may take. The ball has started rolling. The ugly facts have been bared. Now it is just a question of time. The congressional coddling of the tobacco industry will become a political liability, and the cigarette, as we know it, will disappear into memory like chicken fat, garter belts and the wire around milk bottle caps.

Until that momentous day arrives (with probably another national holiday and three-day weekend to commemorate it), we need to help today's smokers realize how much disturbance they are causing. With patient education, the quality of life can be improved for everyone.

Actually, I have a considerable amount of pity for smokers. For the most part, they are addicted to this habit. Even the tobacco company executives have finally been up-front in admitting this. Smokers cannot easily break this habit even if they want to. Witness the umpteen "pacifiers" in the drugstore, the endless stop-smoking clinics and classes, the hypnotists, patches, and balls behind the ears. Smokers, sadly, have to read what their habit is doing to their bodies on a daily basis, and how it is shortening their lives. Smokers have to huddle outside buildings to have their puff, or sit at the edges of restaurants reserved for rest rooms, phone booths, and stacks of highchairs.

After years of doing their thing, smokers are now the object of persecution (as well as numerous surveys!) Their habit has become the focus of gigantic lawsuits. Victims of a habit that grips them, they are now an identifiable "group" or "minority" which is not particularly well esteemed. Hence, my feeling of sadness for their situation.

What totally irritates me, though, about smokers is their *lack of awareness*. They are surprisingly oblivious of the impact they make on the people around them. I was eating with my wife in a restaurant in an unidentified country in Europe. I was somewhat miffed because there was a cloud of steady smoke coming from a man at the next table, preventing me from tasting my pricey food. After tolerating a smoked fruit cup, smoked soup, and a smoked main dish, I summoned up the nerve to salvage my dessert and speak to the perpetrator. He didn't speak English too well, but he finally understood my partially pantomimed message that his smoking was causing me a problem with my meal, and could he please stop until I finished eating.

His reaction and response to me was dumbfounding and totally surprising. He motioned to the wall of the restaurant and asked, "Where does it say that I cannot smoke?" Looking me straight in the eye, he was totally unconcerned that he was causing a fellow human being direct discomfort. As long as his act did not violate any regulation he would cheerfully continue what he was doing. That was his defense. It was as though I did not exist and my plea was not coming from a living person with feelings.

Smokers are unaware about so many aspects of their habit. The endless sea of butts, made nondegradable by their filters, are outright filth. Yet immaculately dressed individuals have no compunction about flicking their finished cigarettes into gardens or urinals or the street, as though it were nothing. These same individuals would meticulously flick a piece of lint off their jackets or dresses or carefully adjust a hair out of place. Cigarette butts are just ordinary litter, like bottle caps, can tabs or dirty tissues, and their presence often diminishes the esthetic enjoyment of a natural setting.

Smokers, regretfully, smell bad. And I would bet dollars to donuts that they are not aware of the extent. Beautifully coiffed and immaculately dressed ladies smell of stale smoke. Their breath is an unpleasant giveaway, like a drinker's breath reeks of alcohol. While it mostly hurts them, it often makes being near them unpleasant.

You cannot get away from smoke in a closed area. The smell spreads. Someone eating, who has trouble with smoke in terms of enjoying his food, cannot escape the smoke except by leaving the room. To divide a given restaurant into "smoking" and "nonsmoking" areas is often a farce. Unless the restaurant has an exhaust system the size of a jet engine, the areas become one and the same. Yet many smokers are oddly unaware of this annoyance that they create for others. When I get frustrated making my point to them, I am always tempted to suggest that they sit in a restaurant just outside the men's room. During years of travel on airplanes whose rear section of rows was designated as "smoking rows," I was often victimized by being assigned a row one or two in front of the cutoff point. It took me forever to remember, when I made my reservations, to not only request a "nonsmoking" seat, but one which was at least six rows forward from the rear of the plane.

When I think of lack of awareness, another situation comes to mind. When our kids were younger, and my wife and I were afraid of second-hand smoke, we asked our visiting friends and relatives not to smoke in our house. If they needed a puff, they should please go outdoors. The scenario was usually the same (and these were people close to us!). They would enjoy their cigarette outside the front door. (It was no small effort to get them to move away from the door. They couldn't imagine that as the door opened and shut, any breeze would carry the smoke right back in.) At the end of the cigarette, they would take one last strong inhale, flick the still burning butt onto my lawn (of course) and charge back into my house. They had no clue that they were smoke saturated, that their next ten exhales smoked out my whole house! Help!

I am reminded of one more item on my list of offenses, although I haven't witnessed it in years. I would be talking to a smoker who had a cigarette in his or her mouth with a long ash tip dangling from the end. The smoker? Unconscious, of course. But I would gradually lose track of the conversation, and totally focus on the ash and where it was heading. Would it scatter down the shirt, tie, and jacket? Would it land on my favorite sofa? Would it plunk to the carpet to singe the fibers? (Ah! Those gorgeous hotel lobby carpets tainted with butt scars.) Always a mess or a fear of mess. Inevitably, the ash tip would miraculously fall into a drink he was holding. The tension would thus end for me and the speaker would continue talking as though nothing happened.

So, my huffing and puffing comrades, I pray for your sake, that you can break this habit and help make this world a better place. Until then, please reassure me from time to time that you can even minutely imagine how your habit affects your partners on this earth. And let's have "no whiffs or butts about it."

⁘ 21 ⁘

Co-existence and Compatibility at the Movies

WATCHING A MOVIE VIDEO at home behind closed doors is a comfortable, inexpensive, everyday family activity. It doesn't impact anyone but yourself and your loved one (or loved ones). It combines the best of all worlds. You can watch a fantastic film. At any point, according to your wish or whim, you can have a snack of any kind, or any odor. You can chew noisily on carrots, popcorn, or peanut brittle. You can open and close the popcorn bag a hundred times. You can talk among the other viewers and ask them to explain what just happened or to repeat a slurred phrase. You can answer the phone, make a phone call, or go the bathroom. You can shift your furniture, put your baby on your lap or make the volume softer or louder. You can smooch with your companion or forget that the movie is on and go about your daily business. All this for two or three dollars per movie, for one person or for the whole Russian army. What a luxury!

It is because of all the above, however, that I have never watched a whole rented video movie in my entire life. Personally, I like to lose myself in a film, as I like to lose myself in a book. I prefer to shut out my entire world and enter the world that the movie director created. I want to feel and see and hear and experience only those sensations that were crafted for me by the makers of the film.

Going on the assumption that those who go to a movie theater are
similar to me, it would seem that the rules in a movie theater would be
much more structured than the freedom of flow in a home environment. And justifiably so. After all, instead of paying top price of two or
three bucks a video (or no bucks from a neighborhood library), the
theater goer has to spring for seven or eight dollars per person plus gas
and tolls and often the hefty price of a babysitter.

So, to my fellow viewers in a movie theater, I would like to address
three areas where we can be kind and considerate of one another. If we
are to make this world a better place for our grandchildren, we have to
be more aware and sensitive. I am appealing for improvement in our
behavior in public theaters. I promise, in return, to respond positively
if you ask me (nicely) to modify *my* behavior in like situations. Just
think. If everyone gave a gentle assent to his neighbor's concern, look
at the happy world we would all enjoy together.

First, let us address eating and talking at the movies. I group them
together because they both cause noisy distractions. If neither are
tolerated at a concert or at an opera to the point where you would
instantly get thrown out if you make a sound, how much more critical
a drop of noise is during a movie. After all, the concert or opera have
either no plot or a two-sentence plot (in my opinion), while every
word of a screenwriter is critical. Unfortunately, those who watch
videos at home are not accustomed to the restrictions imposed (volun-
tarily) in a theater. How wonderful it would be if every response to the
appeal of your "SH-SH," (which happens to be the shortest and the
quietest though not most diplomatic appeal you have available) would
be a rapidly whispered, "Oh, I'm awfully sorry."

What's the favorite food sold at a movie theater concession stand?
Of all things, popcorn! This noisy snack is sold in incredibly sized
portions in an atmosphere that begs for silence. A normal person in his
own home would never dream of consuming the same wash bucket

size tubful of popcorn that he tantalizingly and slowly eats at a movie. Before every showing, the theater owners are guilty of giving that computerized, animated, mixed message to the members of the audience. It says at the same time, "Be quiet, no talking," and "Patronize our refreshment stand" (with its load of crunchies). Maybe their offerings of sweets and snacks could feature the less audible.

So, again, awareness, and the desire to please one's fellow human beings, is the running theme. Every individual knows how to accomplish the kindness that is called for and the restraint that would make everyone happy. If this is the motivation, then a "SH-SH" is really not a rebuke or a threat to one's ego or an embarrassment in front of one's girlfriend. It's just a reminder, an appeal, a plea for your consideration. After all, if you refuse to cooperate, there is no place else for the "shusher" to watch the movie. He really and truly is at your mercy.

A second, albeit brief, opportunity for goodness to our fellow moviegoers occurs as you are leaving the theater. You have just sat through the worst movie of your lifetime. It was a movie raved about by your close friends, who even went so far as to say that they hadn't laughed this much in years. You had given up important alternate plans in order to see this film. It had, in your estimation, no plot, no message, no pretty people to look at, and no movement. It was a disjointed potpourri of silly slapstick humor that would try the patience of a kindergarten child. You are seething. You are restless. You are just itching for an outlet for your frustration. As you leave the inner lobby of the theater, you are about to pass those in the outer lobby, standing on line waiting to fill the seats of the movie you have just vacated. The waiting crowds of people look at you searchingly for a comment, a hand signal, a facial expression, an indication from you as to what you thought about the film.

This is the very moment of the test of your character. Despite your inner fury, you must be fair to those about to enter. They have already paid the aforementioned ticket price, gas tolls and baby sitter costs. Your facial message will set up the mood that will usher them inside. The easiest, most natural thing for you to do is to make comments, like "Do yourself a favor and get your money back," or "What an awful waste of two hours." Don't roll your eyes and look heavenward. Don't shake your head or stick your forefinger down your throat to feign inducing vomiting. The people waiting in line have a right to go to their seats with a sense of optimism and anticipation. Don't spoil it for them. Keep a pleasant, friendly smile. "How was it?" some yell toward you. You just nod with a gentle grin as you quickly pass by their ranks. They, after all, may have very different tastes than you. They may be in a better mood or more rested than you. They might just adore this film, as did your own friends. They may love any kind of comedy, and go to the movies just to relax.

The key here is that, for a fleeting moment, they are dependent on you and any kindness you have within you. Don't taint their experience. Don't vent your frustration on them. Be fair, be gentle, be neutral. The objective ultimate evaluation of this feature film, not that it really makes a difference, will be on public record in the final sales figures and in the consensus of movie critics reviews. Your job is merely to keep this waiting bunch in the lobby happy and hopeful.

Issue number three for me occurs as a movie ends when I am at a theater with a group of friends. At the end of the final scene, there appears on the screen the rolling cast of characters or just simply "The End." It is over. I have just seen an intense film. The love story has overwhelmed me. The sadness has stirred me to the point of tears. For two hours, I was tossed through the emotional roller coaster created by the screenwriter and director. I have a lump in my throat. I am somewhat teary-eyed. I try to absorb my thoughts and feelings. What will happen to the heroine now? Will she ever recover from this tragedy? Will the children ever find out in later years? How sad! I sit there limply as the rolling list of bit actors and supportive crew continues. All I can do is stare. Vaguely, I come to my senses and become aware of people putting on their coats and walking to the exit.

Through my haze, I suddenly hear a staccato-like chatter coming from my own group of friends.

"Boy, am I disappointed!"

"This doesn't begin to compare to the book."

"Whose idea was it to see this junk?"

"I figured out the ending during the first five minutes of the movie."

"Isn't he just gorgeous?"

"This is no better than any cheap soap opera."

"I saw the original version of this movie in 1960 and this one doesn't begin to compare."

"Could you understand what he was talking about with that thick accent?"

"If I wanted to be this depressed, I would have stayed home."

"Can you imagine, $7.50 for a movie ticket and they wouldn't take my Visa card?"

"I can't let my kids see this picture."

"What's this country coming to anyway?"

"Where's my scarf? Did anyone see my scarf?"

My bubble has been rudely busted. I needed silence for a while. I needed peace. The end of a movie is similar to the end of an emotional dream. You need to sift through the pieces and let everything fall into place. You have to resurface slowly to avoid getting the bends. You have to let the reality of the here and now slowly and gently reappear in your psyche. You need for the wounds of your heart to fade into the background.

What I am appealing for, once again, is awareness of the feelings of others. In a specific sense, there ought to be a moratorium of one to ten minutes where nobody talks when a movie ends. Nobody! Absolute silence! That would do it for me. No one likes to be awakened from a deep sleep by the loud bell of an alarm clock. This is no different. Let that ten-minute moratorium be like my alarm clock's snooze button. Give me my ten minutes to rejoin the world, please!

·-· **22** ·-·

Holier Than Thou

THERE IS AN OLD STORY of a man who buys a three-piece suit, one jacket and two pair of pants. The idea is that if anything happens to one of the pair of pants, the other becomes a backup pair. And, of course, he burns a cigarette hole in the jacket.

Occasionally, I have sat in a row in a theater or a place of worship and something dreadful has happened. On one occasion, in shifting my position, I was startled by a tearing sound. I grabbed my leg reflexively to inspect the damage. Unbelievably, there was a tear in this, my best suit. I ran my hand across the back of the bench in front of me and found the incriminating evidence. There, a sharp nail head was protruding, maybe a quarter of an inch at most, out of a seam in the wood. It was almost invisible to the naked eye, like a pothole waiting, hardly visible, to break a car axle or dislodge a hubcap, this was a clothing pothole. It was easily capable of tearing a priceless dress or a one-of-a-kind made-to-order outfit.

I was in a uniquely powerful position. There were untold masses of potential fellow sitters on this seat all in danger of snagging good clothing. They were unaware of the hidden danger, and they were dependent on me.

In my new role as seat guardian for myself and others, I must go right over to the maintenance engineer of the establishment, and ask him to not only fix this nail, but to check all the seating for more of the same. Maybe the culprit was the result of a sloppy installation. Maybe it was from warping wood. Either way, however inconvenient for me, I must report the problem and be certain that the individual hearing my request is the proper one to follow up on it.

So much for holy thoughts!

ᐧᐧ 23 ᐧᐧ

Where Your Help Is Needed

THE WORLD NEEDS lots of help in this new century. As we have discussed, the improvement will come, not in great upheavals or revolutions, but rather in tiny little steps like a toddler developing its ability to walk. These steps will be between persons—giving, sharing, helping, supporting, and encouraging one another. The good feeling that this will bring about will transform us from the sometimes-extreme competitive, possessive, aggressive, survival mentality of the animal world to a higher level of love, compassion, and even self-sacrifice.

The previous chapters spell out typical scenarios, which we can easily relate to in our daily lives. However, I am challenged as to what to do to change one area—the long lines leading into ladies' powder rooms in theaters and public buildings, lines that extend out into the lobby and just don't seem to move.

Picture, if you will, a fifteen-minute intermission in a Broadway play. Everyone runs downstairs to the lower lobby to the restrooms. All the men chatter away, smile, enter the men's room in droves. Quickly, they exit in droves, like a rotating assembly line. They happily chug up the stairs and still have ten minutes of the break between acts to eat or socialize. (For those purists, it is true that the older the male patron whose increasing age necessitates this lavatory break, the slower his rotation and his chug back up the stairs.)

The women? Chatting away, they descend these same steps toward the ladies' room. Unlike men, they never exhibit any rush or urgency. When they get to the promised land, they get in line. There are probably five women inside and forty waiting outside. I wonder if there is any kind of statistical study on what percentage of women successfully enter the lavatory compared with those that don't.

In no time at all, the house lights start flickering, announcing the imminent beginning of Act II. And those in line? No problem, they are smiling and talking away. Do they stay in line and miss the first twenty minutes of the second act or do they cheerfully return to their seats, never giving an inkling or a clue to their friends as to whether they made it to the ladies' room or not? Who knows? Is anyone unhappy about all this? Well, I am!

There is something dreadfully wrong here. The current system has always failed. Without getting graphic, the various factors involved are incompatible and are not working. The number of stalls, the required time, the tendency of well-dressed women in a theater to take their time, and the outside time limits for reasonable intermission—all seem to work against each other. Perhaps a public subcommittee needs to be established. (Let's call it "Intermission Impossible.")

⸭ **24** ⸭

Hair Rights

PICTURE THIS SCENARIO. It is a rainy Wednesday afternoon and my wife and I have two theater tickets for a Broadway matinee. She waits for me in the lobby. I have just run three blocks in the rain from a parking lot near the Hudson River to save $4.00 on the parking fee. I am wet and worried about getting there by curtain time. I arrive. My wife and I are shown to our seats. It is warm in the theater. I remove my raincoat and fold it up on my lap. The seats feel tiny. The space between the rows seems nonexistent. I'm feeling claustrophobic. I am hot and sweating. My wife is relaxed and happy. She is smaller than I am, not overweight like I am, and prefers the theater somewhat warm rather than chilly. The big fellow to my left overflows the one-inch armrest. I am trapped.

The curtain rises and I try like the dickens to settle down. After all, these tickets, even though purchased through a TKTS discount, [See, even company names are abbreviated!] are not inexpensive. It is then that I notice the last straw. There is a young woman sitting in front of me who has long curly straggly hair that extends down almost into my lap. I am about to go crazy. Doesn't my ticket give me the "air rights" up to the seat in front of Me? Isn't this woman aware that this large volume of messy hair has to go *someplace?* Where does she picture it is? She is facing forward enjoying the show, oblivious. If she had a pet Chihuahua on a leash and she sat down on a theater seat, she would be aware that the dog has to be *someplace*. The space around me is closing in further. The hair is literally right in front of my nose. What to do? I look around for an escape. Nothing doing. I am in the center of a row with eight focused people on each side of me.

What are my options? Is it uncouth to bend forward and whisper to the young lady that her hair is causing me a problem and is violating what must certainly be one of my constitutional rights? What exactly should I say? Will saying *anything* provoke a dozen "SH-SH-SH's" all around me? Will she scream angrily at me causing a huge commotion? Will she say, "What did you say?" and force me to repeat myself even louder? Will she go crazy and ask her date to turn around and smash me?

And what words shall I use?

"Miss, your ugly hair is in my lap."

"Miss, could you just lean forward throughout the entire show because your hair is making me feel too crowded in my seat?"

"Miss, could you gather all that hair into your blouse or jacket so that at least it's confined?"

"Miss, have you ever heard of a barrette?"

"Miss, could you curl all that stuff around your neck so that it extends in front of you?"

Shall I rather be devious or dishonest in my question?

"Miss, I think you dropped something under your seat," hoping that after her shifting forward to look down, her hair would end up between her and the seat.

"Miss, could you tap the shoulder of the fellow in front of you. He dropped something."

Maybe that would accomplish the same thing.

Shall I bother my wonderful wife and share my problem with her, tell her I am smothering to death, and tell her that I am in desperate need of her ingenuity and assistance? Or, if I say something to her during a critical moment of the play, when she is so focused, will I end up causing a first fuss before the inevitable second fuss?

The world needs more giving people, more gentle people, more tolerant people, and less confrontational people. I therefore resolve the problem by getting up, slithering out of my row, trying to be as least disruptive as possible, and head out into the lobby. There, I can undo some buttons, cool off a little and collect my thoughts. Maybe I could check my overcoat and jacket. I will get a little drink of water, walk around a bit, even stick my nose out the outer front door to get some fresh air into my lungs.

After a while, my sanity returns. I return to my center seat from the other direction, trying to minimize the disturbance to my fellow moviegoers. Lo and behold! The huge expanse of hair has now disappeared between her and the seat. And it doesn't look so bad after all. (Now I just have to hope that the fellow in front of her does *not* drop something, possibly causing a fatal shift of the hair owner's body.)

All in all, I may have missed out on five minutes of theater. (Figuring at a dollar a minute, that's only about five bucks). If the playwright is worth his salt, I will make up what I missed without any problem. Most of all, with my self-restraint, I have improved the world one tiny notch. To my wife and my fellow theater-goers, I am just another pleasant face in the crowd, co-existing with my fellow human beings in a tolerant, pleasing manner.

··· 25 ···

Lipstick on Her Teeth

WE'VE ALL GONE to a wedding or a lecture or a concert and met an acquaintance there, of the female sort, with lipstick on her teeth. Maybe she was distracted during its application. What to do? If it is a sister or daughter or mate, obviously you point to her teeth quickly to get her to correct the red on white. But what if it's a casual acquaintance, a teacher, a spiritual leader, a performer?

Do you reason that women are women and that, since most females wearing lipstick are embarrassed by the error, the quicker you fix the situation, the smaller the number of viewers of the mess? Or, do you hope that sooner or later this lady (actually, with so many men wearing earrings and cologne these days, can lipstick be far behind?) will pass by a mirror, calculate that nobody yet has noticed her red teeth, fix the situation quickly, and be relieved that she was the first one to notice it.

What's at stake here? A woman's pride. A woman's appearance is high on the list of her priorities. After she has worn herself out getting a dress that hides all the perceived negative shapes of her body, after two hours at the hairdresser, after getting her nails done, and after dyeing her shoes to match her dress, it's an awful shame to ruin it all with a big welcoming red and white smile.

My vote? Once you have attained enough self-confidence through life experience and are old enough to have seen far worse problems, it's really easy. As fast as you notice it, point to her teeth privately and pantomime rubbing it off. She'll instantly know what that means because, for sure, this has happened before. And, after all, it could be worse. It could be a big piece of spinach caught between her teeth throughout a two-hour dignitary's luncheon.

·· 26 ··

Gapitis

I KNEW that the lipstick question was the easy one, compared to this.

You are in a room with people and notice a woman whose blouse button has opened or fallen off. Again, the question comes up? Do you try immediately to buttonhole (pun intended) the unaware victim as rapidly as possible to minimize the exposure time? Do you stand back and enjoy the situation, reasoning that "all's fair in love and buttons"? Or, because this is a touchy (no pun intended) subject, leave it to someone else or to circumstance to deal with it?

In struggling to make this world a better place for my grandchildren, I will cast no vote here. I think the answer will lie in the aggregate of answers to the following questions that pinpoint (pun intended) the specifics of the scenario:

1. Am I, who am faced with this world-improving responsibility, male or female?
2. Am I married or not?
3. How many people are in the room?
4. Are there great refreshments in the room as an alternative?
5. What's underneath the gap?
6. Is my mate or spiritual leader in the vicinity?
7. Do I tend to stutter in predicaments of this sort?
8. Is *her* mate in the room?
9. How big is he?
10. Is there lipstick on her teeth as well?

··· 27 ···

Garlic?

THEY SAY GARLIC is wonderful for your health, a miracle wonder food. Garlic enhances metabolism. Garlic increases sexual function. Garlic increases the absorption of vitamins. Garlic prevents parasites. Garlic slows the process of aging. Garlic adds incredible flavor to virtually all foods. Garlic is natural.

As the father skunk said to the baby skunk, "I'm giving odors around here." (My apologies to all the garlic growers.) Eating garlic, in most cases, causes an awful mouth odor. Plain and simple, garlic stinks. I can smell the breath of someone who has recently eaten pizza with garlic a hundred feet away. I used to tell my children that while still in my car, driving home from work, I could tell if they ate falafel or chumus that day.

Clients come into my office eight o'clock in the morning reeking with foul breath. What have they possibly eaten so early in the day? Whatever happened to Corn Flakes?

I've observed lovely, elegant women, magnificently coiffed, impeccably dressed from head to toe, wearing fifty-dollars-an-ounce perfume, with a mouth odor resembling the local landfill. How can they be so unaware?

Garlic is horrible for your romantic health. How can you kiss someone who smells so bad? Kissing is an important daily ingredient for loving warmth between a man and his wife. "But," protest the garlic fans, "if we both have garlic breath, then everything is okay." That's got to be the oddest observation ever. That's like saying, "She's repulsive. So if I too am repulsive, then we can enjoy mutual repulsiveness."

So if you must have your daily garlic fix, take it by injection or by pill. [Dare I suggest by suppository?] If you have no consideration for the human population who cohabit the earth with you, at least be merciful with the woman you love. Keep your breath kissing sweet, please!

· 28 ·

Here's the Scoop

HOW MANY OF US share a toothbrush with a spouse or a dear one? How many of us share a bath towel? These two questions elicit a wide variety of responses. Some say that sharing a toothbrush or a towel is something they do without even thinking about it. It's like kissing or shaking hands. Then some say, "Well, if I forgot my toothbrush or towel, I guess it would be okay. However, I really prefer my own." Lastly, I imagine a whole group vehemently stating in unison, "What? How absolutely yucky! Never!"

Why the variety of answers? It's because we all have a sensitivity meter that dictates how comfortable we are sharing personal things.

How about sleeping on bed sheets used even once by someone else? How about using someone else's lipstick? Or razor? Or underarm deodorant? How about reading a newspaper after someone else is finished with it and has more or less folded it back to its original form? How about borrowing someone else's pair of socks? How about sharing someone else's sweaty baseball glove? What about a group drinking out of the same beer can or soft drink bottle?

How about a friend using your camcorder? Or wearing your favorite hat? Or bringing a salad that she made to share with you?

How about a drinking glass? Picture a group sitting around the dining room table having dinner. Someone wants some soda. He reaches for the glass at his setting. There are some that grab the nearest glass and just start pouring. There are others who first go through a series of very methodical steps. They reach for the glass, inspect it, and hold it up to the light. Only if they are totally satisfied that no one else has touched their glass or that a crumb hasn't inadvertently fallen into it do they proceed to pour their drink. Different strokes for different folks. Some are fussy to the "nth" degree. Some couldn't care less.

Imagine a bowl of cantaloupe and honeydew melon pieces, with a serving spoon, placed in the center of a table. How critical is it for each person around the table to use the serving spoon to transfer some of the fruit to his or her individual dessert plate? Can an individual use his own fork as a serving utensil to transfer said fruit to his own plate? Can a person take his own fork, stab one piece of melon and put it directly into his mouth? Can he do this over and over, reasoning that his used fork never touches any food but that which goes directly into his mouth?

Is this an issue of good manners or cleanliness or both?

How about a bowl of pistachio nuts on the table? What everyone seems to do is to take a few with his hand to his own plate. He then holds one nut in his hand, puts it to his mouth, pries open the shell with his teeth, eats the kernel, and piles the now empty shells onto his plate. After touching the used nut shells, can he reach back with this same hand into the serving bowl of nuts? Is there ever a scoop provided in the bowl for the non-hand transfer of a bunch of nuts onto one's own plate? I, for one, have never seen such a scoop.

Consider a bowl of salad. Must one use the serving utensils provided for transferring a portion of salad onto his own plate? Can someone, during a lull between courses, during some humorous chit chat, grab a piece of lettuce from the edge of the serving bowl with his fingers and stick it directly into his mouth?

Is this all about Emily Post manners? Or is it all about saliva? Or is the essence of it all the preservation of one's space? "Who cares?" one might ask. The problem is that some people do care and have a problem. They might not even have a problem that is logical. Some might share a hairbrush without thinking, but faint when they see a friend with saliva-wet fingers go back and forth into a dish of salted peanuts. And vice-versa. Someone who eats food off others' plates with a smile might gag if he walks into his hostess's kitchen and see her lick her fingers while she's icing a cake.

The moral of the story is that everyone is fussy and sensitive in certain areas. This fastidiousness is easily taken care of when one is alone. However, when one is in a social situation, where one's actions impact another, it is not so easy. Situations of togetherness around food become partnerships of sorts, where one's good feeling is dependent on someone else's habits or levels of sensitivity.

What is the bottom line? Well, if, for example, a bar-restaurant allows smoking in some sections and it filters through into the whole area, sensitive nonsmokers have a big problem while they're eating. Whereas the smoker has a choice of smoking or not, the nonsmoker has no place to go short of leaving the building. He cannot turn off the smell of smoke. He is literally dependent on having no one smoke. True, he could eat at home or go to hypnosis therapy to turn off sensitivity to smoke, but when he is there in that restaurant he is stuck.

The transfer of saliva, personal manners and individual space are the same issues in community eating. Those not sensitive chew and giggle and have a good time. Those blessed (cursed?) with protective fussiness are in trouble.

The decision must be made to accommodate sensitive individuals. What we do when we are alone is totally different from the obligation we have when we are partners with others. Hosts and hostesses should provide clearly visible serving spoons and forks with their serving bowls, as well as individual plates to which food can be transferred.

Those serving utensils should not be limited to the obvious courses, such as pasta or salads. They should likewise be provided for condiments and desserts such as sliced pickles and melon pieces. Large bunches of grapes should be divided into small clusters beforehand so that one can take his little portion without handling the large bunch.

Lastly, what to do with bowls of peanuts or raisins or chocolate bits or pistachio nuts or Good N'Plenty? (Remember them?) It's simple. Little scoops or ladles should be provided. No more wet fingers going back into the bowl. No more honor system. We must allow for the fastidious among us to have a feeling of cleanliness and neatness. In time, hopefully, it will become the accepted norm.

Does all this have any effect on our foreign policy? Or reducing the world's destitute and poor? Definitely not. Remember, though, to make this world a better place, the quality of life among us will be upgraded by tiny frequent upward steps, not big glacier movements every ten million years. Who knows? The serving spoon could hold the key to future world peace.

Excuse me, please, but can you pass me the dish of nuts and raisins. I'm in the mood for a little scoopful.

⁓ 29 ⁓

Cleanliness versus Employment

WHENEVER I EXIT a supermarket, I roll the shopping cart to my car in the parking lot and transfer the full bags of groceries onto my back seat. I invariably roll the now empty cart to an area between two parking spots where it seems to not interfere with any movement of cars. Do I return it to the little designated island where all the carts are lined up? No. Why not? Because leaving my shopping cart around somewhat sloppily does not seem to cause a problem. Besides, everyone does it. Besides, there is always an attendant somewhere in this vast lot who is collecting carts and walking them, telescoped, to the collecting area, and his employment is dependent on being needed.

In my teens, my summer employment was that of a beachcomber. I worked weekday mornings from 6:00 A.M. to noon in Long Beach, Long Island. I was a member of a crew of six to twelve young men who walked the beach spread out in a line from the boardwalk to the water. We walked from the midpoint of Long Beach to each end on alternate days. Since poles with nails in them were forbidden, we walked and picked up trash with our hands, depositing it into a round wooden vegetable basket we were alternately carrying and dragging. We picked up soda cans, newspapers, cardboard boxes and just about everything imaginable. The pay was good—it helped me save up for college—and, at least for six hours each day, my parents could count on my being productive and staying out of trouble.

At clothing stores, there is an employee whose job all day, apparently, is to go into the fitting and dressing rooms to pick up the tried-on clothes left on benches or hooks by customers. The clothes have to be folded again neatly, matched up with its mate if a suit, its pockets checked for accidentally left items, and eventually hung up again on the proper rack in the proper department.

I have often wondered what would happen if I took the time to roll my shopping cart to the exact area that the posted signs request of me? And what if everyone did the same? Would that poor attendant be out of a job? What an awful thought. Maybe he would be reassigned to a different job at the supermarket. His new job might be to restock the enormous number of items sloppily left all around the checkout counters by people who changed their minds the last minute (or who couldn't find the matching coupon). He would take all these rejects painstakingly back to their assigned spots on the shelves. But . . . what if the market already has someone doing this other work? Would the manager find him still another job or would he be fired?

In the library, people browse through books before checking them out. They use reference books for some kind of project. They copy some pages with the copier. What happens to these books that are used and not checked out? [Someone told me many, many years ago that you are not supposed to place them back on the bookshelf so you don't commit the mortal sin of putting them back in the wrong place!] People leave the books on tables, chairs, edge of the shelves, copiers, and window sills. Any and every surface is used. What happens to them? A part-time student is hired to collect them onto rolling carts from which they are carefully returned to the exact numerical location from whence they came.

Again, what would happen if every library patron did a very simple thing? They put a little piece of paper between the two books on either side of the book they are removing. If they decide not to check out the book, they use the sequential number on the back of the book and the little piece of paper, assuming it's still there, to return the book unmistakably back to its proper place on the shelf. Ah, but what about the sweet part-time schoolgirl counting on the few dollars she makes every week to help her struggling family? What if it were your daughter or granddaughter? Would she be fired? Or would she be assigned to other duties like restacking books left in the book drop by library users, the majority of whom use the book drop to save the few steps from the outside of the entrance to the library desk?

What about my job? Here I was, counting on my biweekly check. What if every beach-goer brought with him or her a plastic garbage bag into which every item of trash were deposited, as required in many state parks and camping grounds. There would be that "Carry-in, carry-out" rule. So simple. Everyone would discard his little trash bag into those big garbage pails at the entrance to the beach. Like mothers discarding their babies' messy diapers. Like pooper-scooper bags used by dog owners who walk their dogs and clean up after them. Will I be let go? Will I be reassigned to truck duty where trucks clean empty lots used by people as dumping ground for their refuse? Can I count on people continuing to stay messy and sloppy?

It is a difficult dilemma. Does the negative behavior of some create employment for others? Is this good or bad? Does it keep the economy flowing? Does the existence of sanitation departments perpetuate the messiness of people or the use of disposables? Does my daily presence as a beach cleaner encourage someone who flings a used soda bottle toward a large garbage pail, but misses—to just leave it there? Am I allowed or really encouraged to leave five library books, or ten for that matter, all over the place, because I know someone is picking up after me?

What if I am in a supermarket line on a busy day just ahead of three customers with filled shopping carts, and I decide that I only need two cans of tomato sauce rather than the three that I put in my cart? Which is better for humanity? To hold up the line to walk the can back to its place in aisle four (or was it aisle five)? Or to hide it among the magazines at the checkout counter, arguing that my messy ways are ensuring the employment of people whose sole job is to clean up after me? Or, . . . is the status of the country's unemployment rate just a rationalization for individuals to pollute and soil every environment they touch?

I don't think I can just let my grandchildren decide on this one. Pollution and discarded trash in any place other than designated containers can *never* be good. It brings the world down. We all need fine-tuning in our daily habits to elevate ourselves to a better quality of life. And what will happen to my friend, the shopping wagon attendant? I am confident that he will do just fine in our cleaner, neater, more considerate existence.

⸙ 30 ⸙

Scissors' Palace

THE ABOVE NAME was seen while passing a barbershop recently. Other clever barbershops I have run across are "Hair Today, Gone Tomorrow" and "A Cut Above the Rest." (The name I penned is "Coiff Medicine.")

Over the years, I have always read during a haircut, either material I brought with me or a magazine from a pile on the barbershop window. (For the last number of years, I have refrained during the procedure because my reading glasses interfere with the movements of the scissors.) I can recall that one day I gave in to my curiosity and took a "men's" magazine for my reading. Needless to say, I was shocked out of my sideburns on the first two pages. The "Letters To The Editor" were more pornographic than any NC-17 rated movie!

At the five-minute mark of my twenty-minute snipping, I happened to look up and noticed the barber looking down at the pages over my shoulder. It gave me an instant fright. Forget about what the barber would think of me, a professional working in the neighborhood, reading this risqué magazine in public. The fright was more graphic. I pictured him forgetting what he was going, thoroughly distracted by one of the magazine pictures and totally losing his concentration. He was holding a long razor! He could cut off my ear by mistake!

I instantly rolled up the magazine and vowed never to open one again. Thereafter, I would read a parenting magazine or a news periodical instead. This might keep his eyes on my head. Can you picture getting sliced open, getting sutured in an emergency room, and having to tell the story of how it happened to curious friends and relatives?

It would be wonderful if the atmosphere of a barbershop would return to that of a palace instead of a tavern. For many years, I took a haircut at an Italian parlor in which four funny extrovert barbers chatted, giggled, argued, cut a little, chatted some more, gave a little snip here and there, and quickly returned to their debate, which was, of course, in Italian and which I did not understand. [Isn't it true that when people are speaking in a language you don't know, it seems as though they are talking twice as fast as you speak at normal speed?]

Invariably, friends of the four barbers would stroll in, come right up next to the working hairdresser and chew his ear off (not literally). So as I sat in my comfortable Caesar's throne with a man cutting my hair and tending my scalp, I had his friend almost leaning on me blabbing away animatedly with the barber who was supposed to be focused on giving me the best haircut possible. One day, when the decibel level of the Italian political debate in my ear reached the intolerable level, I finally blurted out: "Can you please move away from my chair and wait with your conversation until I am finished so that I can my enjoy my haircut?"

The friend did promptly move away and the barber patted my shoulder and murmured "I'm sorry." Of course, I felt very guilty because these are all are adorable and fun-loving guys.

I do think of a haircut as I do of a massage or a facial. It is a personal experience, someone working by hand on your body. Sometimes, it is a very quiet experience. Sometimes, it is filled with active interesting conversations between snipper and snippee. In fact, many individuals can't wait for their chit-chat with the barber just as they enjoy the exchange with their favorite bartenders. Sometimes, the best new jokes come from these fun sessions. The key, though, is that the degree of dialogue should be chosen by the paying customer, not the proprietor.

My barber? I like him because he leaves the amount of talking to me. Most of the time, I arrive and greet him pleasantly. We exchange pleasantries. I then close my eyes and enjoy my silent haircut until he is finished. I am pleased with his expertise. I benefit from a delightful relaxation in an action-packed day. Caesar has enjoyed his palace, *his* way.

·⁖· 31 ·⁖·

Honesty in Business

"THANK YOU," said the wealthy matron standing up at the end of the meeting. "Here is $100. I have confidence that with you as my new attorney, the matter will be taken care of satisfactorily." She handed the attorney the crisp new $100 bill, turned, and left his office. The lawyer waved goodbye, started to put the money into his wallet, but abruptly stopped. Upon careful scrutiny, he noticed that the lady did not leave him $100 as she stated. There were actually two $100 bills stuck together. He immediately had an ethical problem . . . should he tell his partner about it?!

This story brings out the frequent dilemma that men and women in business confront in their daily work: the profit motive versus integrity. They certainly should be lofty and up front with their employers, employees and co-workers. They owe their highest level of obligation, though, to their clients and customers. Regardless of the shrewdness of the customer and the enormous amount of information available today on the Internet, the simple fact is that you cannot beat a man in *his* game. A real businessman (or businesswoman) knows the real quality and dependability of his product. He knows its source and ingredients. He knows its life expectancy. He knows the small print in the law. He knows the real expiration date. Whether he is selling diamonds or avocados or weight-reducing diets, he generally has the advantage in any situation. With this comes the awesome responsibility of the trust that is vested in him by his fellow human beings.

Profit is the reason people join most professions and businesses. Anyone who takes the risk and makes the investment to own a practice or business is certainly entitled to financial gain. If a fur manufacturer makes a fur coat in his factory for "x" dollars, he may determine any price he wants to sell it for. The market will determine whether the price he sets will attract customers. There are documented average fees available to clients and customers for services rendered, whether those of a dentist, a gardener, a dry cleaner or a home decorator. The consumer makes his choice, and the laws of supply and demand determine the market. The merchant also makes his choice as to how high a price he asks for his product. All this is well and good.

Where ethics and morality kick in as an important factor is in the quality of the goods or service provided. The average consumer is often blind to the true nature of the product. He depends on the providers in so many instances. I recently purchased a case of clementines at a fruit stand. The case was inexpensive and the orange fruit looked great. Sad to say, the clementines under the top visible layer were very soft and borderline spoiled. In this case, the sale price was agreeable to vender and purchaser. The hidden poor quality of the product left me as the unfortunate loser.

In the case of fruit, the loss is mostly a temporary annoyance. How much more is the penalty when a critical product is involved. The manufacturer of a crib can cause a disastrous calamity if a defective part could injure a new baby. Likewise, the manufacturer of airplane hardware has the lives of hundreds of passengers dependent on his credibility on every flight. An airbag manufacturer, a drug company, a maker of fire-resistant clothing, a baby food bottler—all have so many lives in their hands. The list is long.

Similarly, the service industry and the professions have the burden of giving their fellow human beings a fair shake. The professionals, like lawyers and physicians and therapists, are well paid because the stakes are high in the work they are doing. There is no room for any dishonesty or cutting corners or even simple incompetence. Service industries like telephone repair, fire-extinguisher maintenance, roofing, exterminating, and automobile repair provide the technical know-how that most of their customers are totally lacking. They must not take advantage. They must, in addition to getting paid, be sure that their trusting client is not getting shortchanged just because he or she is dependent on them.

Sadly, the newspapers are full of scams and fraud in the business world. Mankind, unfortunately, has not been created with enough natural safeguards from within to control the passion for financial gain. Ethics in the market place is such a critical factor in the quality of life among us. It should be harped upon in the home for kids to learn from a very early age. It should be hammered away frequently in schools. It should be a frequent subject of religious sermons and seminars. Oddly, this subject seems to slip through the cracks and, compared to the more dramatic problems like alcohol and abuse, is often neglected.

They tell the story of the government inspector who slapped a stiff fine on a butcher, charging him with false advertising. Said the inspector: "You advertise that you are selling rabbit burgers, but our laboratory found that the burgers are almost all horsemeat, rather than the fifty percent rabbit meat that the law requires for such advertising." "But," protested the butcher, "they are fifty percent rabbit and fifty percent horse. One rabbit and one horse!"

My grandchildren need a safe world to live in and a safe business climate to deal with. We must work together to elevate ourselves spiritually in this area.

┄ **32** ┄

Water Meter versus No Water Meter

WHY MUST MY INTEGRITY and my honesty be subjected to constant tests? I am a weak mortal. I am frail. As my father used to say, "I can resist everything except temptation!" Alas, these ethical challenges keep appearing on my scene, and I have to deal with them.

In my house, I have a water meter. I pay for water by the drop. I pay for every use of water. Unfortunately, I also pay for every unnecessary use of water—any drip from any faucet. A toilet that has the annoying habit of constantly running when not being used. A lawn sprinkler head that doesn't completely shut off when the timer closes the other heads. A garden hose with old washers that cause water to spray out both ends when the water is turned on.

I think about water a lot, especially in times of shortage. I have to make decisions every day that I really don't want to make, usually because the water meter is ticking relentlessly. If I want a drink of cold water from the tap, shall I run the water a long time until it gets colder, or do I settle for a lukewarm drink to save pennies? If I blow my nose, do I toss the used tissue into a waste paper basket or do I toss it into the toilet and flush? What does it cost me?

When I wash a dirty pot in the sink after a meal, how clean must it really be? If it has the slightest feeling of grease, do I keep washing or call it a draw? When I clean a bathtub that only I use, how hard do I try? When a deliveryman asks for a drink of water, do I offer him a full glass? When the kettle finishes boiling the water for my nightly cup of tea, how quickly do I shut it off? When I brush my teeth, do I keep the water running? How many times do I rinse my mouth? Saving money on water is no different than clipping supermarket coupons or comparison shopping for a tank of gas.

If, out of curiosity, you get scientific and call the water company to inquire about the cost of normal uses of water, like taking a shower or flushing a toilet, be prepared. First of all, you are to be considered lucky if you don't get put on hold for half an hour. If you do get a live person (after pressing "1" for a touch-tone phone, "3" for a non-emergency service question, and then "5" if you don't want the call recorded) you probably won't get a satisfactory answer any way.

Now, you may ask, where is that great big morality challenge to my character that I began with? The answer is that at my office, as opposed to at my home, the water is not metered. I pay by the year, regardless of how much I use. I don't pay for every drop or every drip. No one is watching me. Do I watch my use of water at work (I use a lot!) as scrupulously as I do in my home? Do I avoid unnecessary waste to the "nth degree"?

Or, conversely, do I luxuriate and lavish myself unnecessarily to balance the nervous attention that I give in my home? How do I avoid the guilt caused by being totally carefree about conserving fresh, pure, potable water when I'm not paying for it?

The water that reaches my office and my home starts out as snow on some upstate mountaintop, melts, and mixes with rain. It runs in streams through rocks and pine needles down the mountainside into picturesque creeks and then flows into huge conduits that head toward

New York City. It is then filtered and fluoridated, chemically treated and pumped throughout the city. It is frequently spot-checked and sampled in environmental laboratories by dozens of inspectors, laboratory technicians and water engineers. Can I really afford to be arrogant and abuse this precious liquid? After all, no one is watching me.

May we all have the strength to do the right thing. After all, the Almighty is always watching us. We are the caretakers of our natural resources. If we want the world to be a better place for our grandchildren, if we want the world to be in good shape for our grandchildren, we should act as though our grandchildren are always in our presence, watching us trustingly.

⚊ 33 ⚊

Bank Vaults are
Anything but Dull

IT MUST BE the seriousness and secretiveness and the foreboding appearance of bank vaults that drive one to find all the silly aspects of these havens in the banking industry. Years of being a safety deposit box customer causes me to grin today whenever the subject is mentioned.

I will tell you a little known secret. The smallest size safety deposit box costs in the neighborhood of twenty to thirty dollars per year. Do you know what you get for this money? (Please don't tell anyone. It's our secret). Not what you guessed, a box to store your valuables and jewelry and important papers. For thirty dollars a year, you have the use of a large or small room with a lock on the door where you can spend at least six hours a day! It is the most incredible bargain in creation. You can do anything behind those closed doors. It is your private office or your private motel room. It is kept neat and clean. It has a paid trained security officer, nearby outside. You will never be disturbed unless, after about five hours in there, they think you died or something. And then it will just be a polite knock to see if everything is OK. It is always air-conditioned, so it's a wonderful place to eat your lunch and read on a steamy summer's day. The furniture, primarily the chair, is always comfortable and luxurious, more so than you can afford for your office. With a briefcase containing a cell phone and a laptop, you can run a thriving business in there.

Some of the rooms are quite large, meant for conferences. Theoretically, you could have a job as a night watchman someplace, working all night. After having breakfast, you could come to your bank at 9:00 A.M. with or without company, and sleep on an inflatable mattress that you bring, or on their plush carpeting, until at least three or maybe four in the afternoon. Now all you need is a place to stay on Sundays and you need not have the expense of a house or an apartment! Remember that no one can take away your privilege once you've paid.

But what about the box? Oh yeah! You could actually keep valuables or money in it if you want. Or you could just keep your makeup kit in there or ketchup samples or your favorite earphones and cassette recorder, or M&M's or a mini-TV or your cellular phone, or old crossword puzzles. Or you can just keep it empty. It's really just your excuse for the use of the room. If you're self-conscious, you can roll up some blank paper to give the box some weight. Anyway, my secret is out.

Which reminds me of the story of the well-dressed man who goes up to the loan officer in a bank and asks for a personal loan.

"How much do you need?" he is asked.

"Ten dollars."

"Ten dollars?"

"That's right."

The banker scratches his head, hands the man a loan application, asking what he is going to leave as security. The man states that he is going to leave him a half-million dollars in municipal bonds as collateral.

"A half million?"

"That's right."

Dumbfounded, the loan officer approves the application, accepts the collateral and collects the two-dollar annual interest rate in advance. The customer heads for the door. "Wait!" shouts the banker to the man, catching up with him. "In thirty years of working in the bank industry, I never ran into anything as strange as this before. If you own a half-million dollars worth of bonds, why, for the love of Pete, do you want to borrow ten dollars?"

"You don't understand," responded the well-dressed man, "Where else can I get a safety deposit box for two dollars a year?"

One of the things that they should teach new trainees for the vault attendant job is never to get too personal or bold with the customers. Friendly, yes. Inquisitive, no. A safety deposit box by its nature implies secrecy and privacy. Even if the vault is busy with customers, no one knows what's in someone else's box. Everything is behind a closed door. The boxes are locked. The gate outside of them is locked. Finally, often the big vault door is clamped shut. "Sh-sh" is the code word. Conversation? Minimal. Maybe "How is the weather outside?" "What time is it?" "Has the rain stopped?"

Unfortunately, in my many years as a vault customer, I have run into the most friendly vault attendants on God's earth. And the loudest. And the most shameless. Across the room, they greet me, personally, at first sight on my arrival. I say absolutely nothing, but their booming voices don't seek answers to their totally embarrassing questions. "How's business, Doc?" "I noticed that you switched to a larger size box, Doc!" "You seem to be coming in almost every day now, Doc!" "Where do you live, Doc?"

Totally self-conscious about my box, this section of the bank, privacy, and anonymity, I shrink into a corner. The embarrassment is overwhelming. It feels as though I am walking around publicly without my pants on. I keep my eyes lowered. I move quickly and grunt occasionally to avoid seeming rude. I try not to meet his eyes. (I don't want him to recognize me in court). I offer a diplomatic quick grin and murmur a soft "Yes, sir." It seems to satisfy my vocal friend. Somehow, he makes the whole visit to the vault a nerve-racking one. When you think of it, these chatty guys ought to be behind the bank's information desk or loan desk. We need some quiet introverts down in the catacombs.

Finally, another piece of juicy information. Several years ago, while waiting for a vault attendant to find the right set of keys to open my box (together with my key), my eyes wandered around the room. After scanning the usual stacks of safety deposit boxes, my eyes alighted on a notice on the wall. It was a set of instructions of what to do if someone were inadvertently locked in the bank, presumably at night, when there would be no response to shouts for help. Next to this notice was a phone. Next to the phone was the *pièce de résistance*, a list of all the bank employees' home phone numbers, from the custodian up to the bank manager.

So there you have it! The next few times you are in the underground room of boxes, memorize a few names and phone numbers, and write them down as soon as you're in your private room. If you are nimble fingered, as soon as the attendant turns away, take a quick close-up Polaroid shot (with no flash, of course). You now have a gold mine in your hands. Have a complaint with the bank? An overcharge on an order of new checks; an error on your statement; an officer not calling you back; a form that you need not getting to you despite numerous phone calls? Want immediate satisfaction? Just call the bank vice president at his home, ten o'clock at night. That will clear his sinuses. You now have power if you feel you have been wronged or neglected.

Now, how, you may wonder, does all this meandering about safety deposit boxes add up to an improvement in the world that my grandchildren will be growing up in? In truth, I cannot come up with an obvious connection. Unless, some day, it will make my grandchildren smile whenever they go into a bank for serious purposes. They will be amused, perhaps forever, thinking that their grandpa had so many adventures in this secretive place. Maybe they in turn will treat their bank officers, guards, tellers and safety deposit attendants with an extra degree of humor and kindness because of it.

·· 34 ··

Marriage versus (In)Significant Others

A 1998 SURVEY concretized an awful fact that everyone was seeing but not realizing. Only 56 percent of adults were married, compared with nearly 75 percent in 1972. Also, the percentage of American households with children dropped to 26 percent in 1998 from 45 percent in the early 1970s. The percentage of households made up of unmarried people with no children was 33 percent, more than double the rate of 1972. Married couples with children younger than eighteen fell to an estimated 36 percent of households in 1997 from 50 percent in 1970.

What has happened to marriage? Where have intact families gone?

Jackie Mason, a superb comic, talked about marriage on a regular basis during his act. With the divorce rate in the country at 50 percent, who in his right mind would marry today? "Can you picture," he posed, "someone going into a new business that had a 50-percent failure rate? Everyone would say this guy is out of his mind!"

I gave a lecture on marriage and dating at a New York City college recently that was intended to teach the skills necessary for an optimum marriage. It became instead a ninety-minute defense of the institution of marriage. My audience, which consisted of faculty and students, questioned the uniqueness of being married. The majority of them were living with someone, their significant other. One young lady proudly shared that she was living with a guy whom she loved, that they had a very close relationship, that they were very happy, and that a piece of paper, a marriage certificate, was not in any way necessary to confirm what they already had. "And," she added, "if we were to become unhappy with each other, we would separate just like married people get divorced."

I grew up in an era when "living together" was referred to as "living in sin," and was unprepared and unrehearsed on how to respond properly to a hostile group. From my upbringing, living with someone was having your cake and eating it too, at least for the male. The few guys we knew that "shacked up" with a girl used to state their party line with a smirk: "If I want to have a salami sandwich, who says I have to buy the whole delicatessen?"

So I responded to my accusers. I equated living with someone outside of wedlock with a merchant renting a store on a day-to-day basis, without a formal lease. This was a risky proposition business-wise. The merchant could build up a tremendous investment in the premises and, at the whim and fancy of the landlord, be thrown out. It is with a formal, legal lease that he has more than a conversational hold on the premises. The retort to my above simile was that when it was over, it was over, legal paper or no legal paper.

I again protested, describing the marriage vow as one more important notch of commitment by the man to the woman than the agreement just to live together. I appealed to the women that it is they who had the most risk in a casual relationship. If the man moves out, he is free and clear of obligation and he can easily find a younger woman. It is the women who, as they age, will have more difficulty finding and attracting (and keeping) a decent male.

The subject of the shrinking percentage of marriages is awesome in its seriousness. Marriage creates the structure of a family. It gives a foundation that provides security to growing children. It gives children their name. It is and always has been the basis of the structure of society. The family unit. Two parents with children living together under one roof. It is incomprehensible that the fabric of society, as we know it, can continue without a resurgence people getting married. It is the small remaining number of intact families today that gives our country the orderliness to function in the optimum way.

The reason for the lowered percentage of intact families today is, as Jackie Mason stated, the awful track record of marriages. The fact that half of marriages end up in divorce (and who knows how many dreadful ones remain intact) is indeed a deterrent to people choosing whether or not to marry. Young people are correct for hesitating and delaying marriage. "My parents had a terrible marriage. How can I expect better?"

The bottom line is that it is imperative that marriage make a comeback. And the only way this can happen is if there is a massive revamping of the education in our schools to include the preparation for marriage. There are a host of skills necessary for enjoying any relationship to the fullest. Even more skills are necessary for living with a person of the opposite sex, a person who comes into marriage with his or her own set of values, expectations, norms, and style of doing things.

My wife and I, terribly smitten with love, had our first argument during our honeymoon over a bowl of cereal.

"I'm going to have a bowl of Rice Krispies," I stated.

"You're going to have a bowl of what?" she asked.

"A bowl of Rice *Krispies*," I said.

"You mean *Rice* Krispies," she retorted.

"No," I protested, "it is Rice *Krispies*."

"You are wrong," she stated, "and if you don't believe me, let's ask ten different people what they think."

There we were, arguing over the pronunciation of a breakfast cereal that we both liked. It was only a difference in *style* by two people brought up in two different households.

Two people are attracted to each other, fall in love, decide to marry within a few months. Just think of it, it takes six months to decide on new wallpaper or the new slipcovers for a sofa. Here are two inexperienced youngsters rushing to make the most important decision of a lifetime. These two kids are each the products of two parents. They meet, carrying not only their own baggage but the baggage of their parents and their parents' parents. There are many differences of values in many different areas to adjust to. There are differences as to where to live. Some people think owning an apartment in Manhattan, New York City is about as special as you can ask for. Others picture a sprawling house in the country with a pond and a few chickens clucking about as heaven. How many children shall we have? How far spaced apart? Do we have the same perception of how they should be brought up? How they should be disciplined? And where should they go to school? How will we set up our work and child care schedules? Are we in agreement over our religious involvement and our place of worship? What are our priorities on charitable giving? How about the household budget? How about recreation priorities, alone time, hobbies, friends?

All these decisions and differences are the work in progress of a healthy marriage. What is necessary is the realization that marriage is for a lifetime. People—like pigeons!—should mate for life. Marriage should be a contract fixed in stone. With this mindset, it is *easier* to deal with problems. Unlike a broken vacuum cleaner that you can toss out, a lifetime relationship *must* be fixed as difficulties arise. Everyone has problems. The difference between good marriages and less good marriages lies in the skills of problem solving. The lifetime partners cannot slam a door and walk out in the middle of an argument. No sulking, no silent treatments. No getting a girlfriend or boyfriend on the side to satisfy the need for warmth and appreciation.

What is needed is the desire to have the best marriage in the whole world. A mate has to be worshiped as a special human being (that's why you chose this individual instead of someone else). Time must be set each and every week to get to know this former stranger. The time must be fixed in stone whether it be a weekend away, a fixed night at a quiet romantic restaurant or a weekly stroll along a bubbly glistening stream. Away from laptops, cellular phones, children (yes, children), remote controls, friends, relatives and any distraction—preferably away from your neighborhood. It is at this weekly rendezvous (you can even check in as Mr. and Mrs. John Doe) that your precious relationship get repaired, renewed, coddled, relished, and stimulated.

"How's it going, honey?"

"What are you working on?"

"How are you feeling about things?"

When things are at absolute peace, the questions can be raised to a higher level.

"Tell me what you dream of doing some day."

"What would be a great vacation spot?"

"How do you think the kids will turn out?"

The time together away from the rest of the world is the time to work on problems between you that cannot be dealt with in the heat of the moment.

"You embarrassed me in front of my friends at the party the other night. That was very unlike you. What brought that on? I was devastated. What were you feeling?"

It is a time to work gently on the behaviors of one's partner that cause tension and resentment. It is an opportunity to really get to know your partner.

"How are you doing with your siblings?"

"Tell me more stories of your childhood."

"What shall I get you for your birthday?"

Marriages, besides requiring work on problems, need ongoing freshening. They have to be kept interesting, growing and stimulating. There have to be ongoing new projects, new relationships, new hobbies and challenges. If, after all, we get bored with our hats or our recipes after a year or two, how are we going to keep two people from getting bored with each other after ten, twenty, forty, or sixty years? The never-ending challenge is to keep fun and humor and youthfulness in the daily routine. The marriage partners have to look for special gifts, unique treats, surprises and opportunities to giggle. They must maintain the dating mentality that excited them when they first met. A night out together is not be taken for granted. It is a date—nice clothing, good planning, prepared energy (and sandwiches), plus a fun attitude.

What is the payback for the seemingly endless daily work? A wonderful reward. It is the privilege of developing and enjoying a soul buddy, a lifetime pal. Here is someone to cuddle with, to hug, to raise children with, to set up a warm home with, to play games with, and to giggle through life with. This is a good friend, someone we like, someone we love. Most people search a lifetime for a fragment of such closeness.

35

Good Marriage, Good Luck

CLOSE MARRIAGE RELATIONSHIPS are not an unreachable ideal. They are achievable by any couple who puts their minds to it. It is true that, besides the constant work demanded to fine-tune them, a good dose of luck and good health never hurts. Good luck is needed because, even with the best foresight, we cannot know how our mate will act in situations down the road when we are ten or thirty years into marriage. We can imagine how a stunning twenty-year-old girl that we are drooling over will be as a mother or grandmother some day but we cannot see for sure while we are courting. Likewise, illness and misfortune can shake up the strongest of us and put a strain on our good intentions. All we can do is work as hard as we can to be loving partners, and pray a lot. However, a husband and wife supporting each other and rooting for each other is the best defense against the sadness and disappointments that touch us all.

Meanwhile, there are two concrete areas that need upgrading to accomplish the necessary return of the high percentage of happily married people that this country desperately needs. As important as spelling or Asian art or medieval literature in the school curricula are courses in relationship skills at all age levels. And there are many. For starters, there can never be too much education on communication skills. How to use words to relate is the basis of any relationship. Children have to be taught early to thank others on a regular basis for what is done for them.

Someday it will be easy for a husband to thank his wife for the rewardless work she does, such as neatly folding up sweaters in his closet. She in turn can thank him properly for surprising her and making the effort to get theater tickets to a special show. Children of all ages (are we ever not children?) must be taught to express their feelings properly. Saying "I feel lousy" might be more adequately expressed with "I feel humiliated" or "disappointed" or "apprehensive" or "embarrassed" or "lonesome" or "betrayed" or "frightened."

Fine-tuning can be taught. Feeling "good" or "great" is okay but could be much improved upon when we are sharing a state of mind with a special partner. What does the generic "great" mean? Better might be the use of words like "relieved" or "proud" or "validated" or "exonerated" or "appreciated." These finely tuned nuances are greatly helpful in understanding what our husbands or wives are experiencing, if we are to be part of the experience.

Listening is a difficult skill, but it is critically needed to achieve closeness with another human being. Frankly, listening is mostly a lost art today. Life is so complex and most people are so self-oriented that to be able to absorb another's travail or joy or unusual experience is really difficult. Most listeners, even those that truly are interested in a speaker's tale, are quickly consumed by their own agenda. As they listen, key words remind them of something *they* have experienced, something they forgot in the oven, something they have to have repaired, or something about *their* children that worries them. The speaker's story is easily lost. Painfully, we come to realize that there are very few people on this earth who not only are truly, truly interested in what we have to say, but have enough self-confidence and focus to put aside their personal thoughts to absorb what we are earnestly trying to tell them.

According to the experts, what is the opposite of speaking? No, it's not listening, as one would expect. It is waiting to speak! How clever and how accurate!

A further refinement on ordinary listening is "active listening" by which the listener hears the emotion behind the verbal message. He then in turn "reflects back" or repeats this emotion, satisfying the speaker that the latter's true message was indeed absorbed.

A husband returns home from work at night and five feet inside his front door smells the odor of meat loaf cooking on the kitchen stove. "Are we having meat loaf for supper *again?*" he shouts to his wife whom he has not even greeted yet.

His actual verbal message only addresses the issue of menu selection. His finely attuned wife knows that this is not the greeting she usually gets from her loving husband. Were she to react defensively to his actual message in an automatic reflex fashion, she would shout back: "If you don't like what I prepared for supper, you can go out to your favorite pub to eat. Don't do me any favors."

Having mastered the skill of active listening, she is able to understand what is going on and respond correctly. "You sound really upset, honey. You must have had a really rough day."

She correctly puts the verbal attack concerning the food in the background. (She knows that her usually voracious hubby will consume anything a cubic foot thick on his plate without even looking at it.) She correctly hears the tension and aggravation in his voice and is able to be an understanding partner rather than a sparring partner.

Besides communication and listening courses, which are useful in all relationships, children should have a full pre-marital curriculum. They must learn the correct expectations of marriage partners. They must learn the obligations. They must consider issues like values, religion, work schedules, child rearing, care of aging parents, friends, location of home, entertainment budget, charitable giving, school selection, sharing premarital assets, etc. They must learn how to take care of their husband and wife—to protect them, to encourage them, to maximize their potential, to share with them, and to make them happy. They must learn the skills of positive reinforcement. They must learn how to compliment their mate daily, to thank them for something and to show physical affection every day. The list goes on.

This list is long and rightfully so. There is much to learn before marriage. The on-the-job learning system that we practice is simply very insufficient for the complexity of two people living together in harmony until death do us part. The divorce rate would drop to a very low level if prospective marriage partners were expert at what they are supposed to be doing from the start. Can I go on the tennis court cold and expect to play well just by willing it? For sure, no. I need lessons. I need drills and exercises. I need constant practice. I need advice from the proven winners. I need successful strategies from experts. I need to develop a court sense. Then, and only then, am I ready to play the game.

Lastly, the government must give monetary incentives for people not only to marry but to assist with the expenses of child rearing and schooling. Until we get the divorce rate down from fifty percent to one percent, many skeptics need tangible financial rewards for choosing the marriage option. Government leaders and legislators must see this as an opportunity to get our country back on track. (The high divorce rate leads to broken families, neglected children, abuse, drugs, crime, welfare and lowered morality.) Tax reductions are in order for joint returns, married housing, schooling, and other family-oriented expenses. Let's get to the promised land regardless of what it takes. Let us do what it takes to raise the level of married adults way above its current ridiculous level of fifty-six percent.

And, certainly, let's encourage our country's leaders to show us by example how to marry, how to raise children, how to pray, how to have lofty thoughts, and how to do the right thing. This is the best path to insure that my grandchildren live in a better world.

·· 36 ··

Religion and
Its Effect on Us

THE PRESENCE OF RELIGION and the observance of its preach-
ings and laws make our lives much richer and more satisfying. It
follows that the more individuals and families grasp the warmth that
religion brings with it, the better a world we would have to live in—
and to leave for our grandchildren.

For the individual, the benefits of religion are multifold. First and
foremost, being under God's control automatically gives us the protection and security of having an Almighty Father. Having such a God
relieves us of having to control every aspect of life. Negative happen-
ings can be attributed to God's master plan, which we may not be able
to fathom, relieving us sometimes of our need to know "Why."
Likewise, faith in God helps us have hope dealing with difficult situations or illnesses or threats to our peace of mind.

Belonging to a religious group makes us a member of a club. We
are not alone. We belong. If we ever travel or move, we can hook up
with new members of our club, and follow their observances and even
use their particular prayer books. Religion reinforces good ethics and
good values, which we already know simply from a compassionate or
humanitarian logic.

Religion, where laws are observed, teaches us self-discipline, that there are wrongs and rights, touchables and untouchables. We learn to enjoy the appetites with which we are created, however, with appropriate limits. We are able to have an inner joy about all the creatures around us—that they are truly miracles, from butterflies to seahorses to baby chicks. Being aware that we are surrounded by God's miracles makes us appreciative of every day and enables us to see that life is a privilege, and that the more we search, the more we can discover new miracles. We see daily occurrences as super special—like conception and childbirth, like the development of a child or a puppy, like the effortless swimming of an otter, like the building of a dam by a beaver.

Religion brings with it the observance of festivals and a year-long schedule of events. These can be celebrated superficially with greeting cards or gifts, or they can be a stimulus for study and research into their history, rituals, and minute laws for interested participants. Even at the simplest level of marking a religious holiday, one is again a member of a club sharing the experience with other club members. Whether it be saying certain prayers or refraining from eating certain foods or wearing a unique article of clothing, the sharing with many others is a form of group therapy and family-like warmth.

There are those who devote a great percentage of their time deep in study. Buying a Christmas tree or getting a holiday sale bargain at the mall are not enough for them. They go to classes and lectures. They go to libraries and other sources for books written by ecumenical scholars and analysts. They derive great satisfaction in understanding the spiritual roots and nuances of day-to-day religious practice in a busy household. They ponder the old customs that were acceptable generations ago juxtaposed on today's newer trends and technological advances. They want to be the finest and most moral human beings possible on this earth and they are willing to put in the time to learn the best way to behave in every daily situation, and to know when there is more than one acceptable choice. And, amongst these more seriously inclined, there are those who graduate to actually become ordained ministers or nuns or rabbis. The majority, though, are those who sit privately, alone or in small groups, to investigate, to delve, to explore.

It is wonderful following an established religion's schedule of events and holidays. It fills up the year! One is always cleaning up the remains of the last festival day and quickly preparing for the rituals of the next. There is always something to think about, to look up, to fine tune. There are recipes to try out and to discard. There are always new products being developed to do things a little easier or a little more accurately than the previous year. There is the characteristic clothing to prepare in advance.

And what about getting the kids ready? They are the future in terms of carrying on these time-honored traditions. Then the home needs work. Whether it be doing the electrical work, preparing for Christmas tree lighting, or removing all the leaven from the house before Passover, everyone is around, fussing and doing. By focusing on holy day accessories and paraphernalia, we never stray too far from God, the source of these special days. We feel more special, more wholesome, more lofty, when our day is filled with ritual-oriented activities.

Then the actual festival day arrives. Everyone is tingling with excitement. There is electricity in the air. The visiting relatives and guests arrive. Work and daily routine get set aside. Out comes the newly purchased clothing. The aroma of holiday cooking and festive cakes fill the air. Everyone is scurrying around, here and there, with last-minute preparations. The incredible bouquet of flowers sits in the center of the dining room table. All the men have that clean look with their fresh haircuts. The young children and grandchildren are flut-tering and dancing around, sensing the upbeat mood of all the adults.

Finally comes the crowning moment, with everyone sitting around the table. The holiday songs, the discussions, the awesome food, the kids' recitations and school projects, the prayers and scholarly insights, (a little arguing and crying), the getting to know the guests, the giggling, the spilled wine, the surprise news (usually of someone being pregnant!), the beautiful candlesticks. One can only pray that this special moment will never end.

So, in the end, religion really brings people together. For those with no families, their fellow congregants are a great potential for togetherness through churches and synagogues. Singles can comingle at lectures, walking tours and concerts, as well as the standard dances and socials. How more comforting and trustable it is to get an introduction at a church or synagogue sponsored event than a pickup at a singles bar. Religious celebrations bring families together. Far-away relatives, out-of-touch relatives, angry relatives have a neutral forum for attempting closeness once again. As they say about skiing, "No pain, no gain." The more meetings, the more chance for rekindled warmth and soothing of the wounds. Everyone is always looking for closeness. There can never be too much of it. New neighbors, visitors to the area, singles, seniors without families are all candidates to join a family for a Sabbath meal. In fact, many churches and synagogues announce at the end of services that anyone needing a meal or a place to stay should contact one of the committee people in charge of this area.

Finally, religion is the best format for keeping individual family members close with one another. The Sabbath meals are a great vehicle for sharing what transpired in each person's life that week. (Simultaneously, the skills of sharing one's feelings and expressing one's self, and most important, of listening, are all fine-tuned—and not to be taken for granted). The members get to know each other better, know what issues they are working on and what relationships are sources of concern. They become conditioned to holiday time being family get together time. This becomes instilled in their children and their children's children. It will keep the children close when they in turn get married and set up their own homes.

The leaders of our communities and our country should show by example and behavior the high priority of religious belonging and observing. Everything comes from the top. Active participation in study and ritual will bring us God's rewards, in His special way. Person to person, soul to soul, here on this earth, we will all grow to be kinder, more compassionate people with a special loyalty and fondness for our fellow human beings.

⊷ 37 ⊷

Good News Programs

THERE IS MUCH TALK about how our TV programming is full of violence and sex. On the assumption that a great percentage of our country's citizens watch a few hours of television every night, it is safe to say that they are exposed to a steady diet of violence and sex. This makes a very strong argument for those who contend that, by virtue of the above exposure, acts of aggressiveness have become more commonplace, even acceptable, as a means of expression. Add violent video games and violent movies to this saturation of everyday aggression seen on TV and it creates an understandable mindset. If something bothers you, just rub it out. A "no" from a woman means "yes." According to the experts, this exposure to violence may also be behind the random shooting at schools and post offices, people arbitrarily pushed in front of moving subway trains, and vengeful acts of arson.

None of the above is new. However, there is another practice evident in our TV programming that, while less obviously damaging, is quietly dangerous nevertheless. The news programs and the talk shows are becoming saturated with *bad* news. Without realizing it, we are getting bombarded with negativity, pessimism and fear. This, in turn, has a tremendous impact on our outlook on daily living. This is bad. That is bad. Everything is bad! Life is just one big pain.

Take an average late-night network news program. The sideshows are the weather, the sports and the commercials. What constitutes the bulk of the subject matter? Trouble and misery. Endless trials of police officers who abuse in some form or another, corruption scandals, infidelity of politicians, embezzlement admissions, malfunctioning school boards, horrible fires, tornadoes and earthquakes that kill hundreds, tragic plane crashes, missing children, random shootings, ozone layer reduction, power outages and train derailments.

Want more? Toxic residue in the ground and in our fish, lightning strike fatalities, rivers flooding and destroying homes, municipal employee strikes, celebrities stricken with cancer, additional foods that are bad for you, food poisonings, outbreaks of tuberculosis, beached whales, automobile recalls, department store bankruptcies, mountain climbing fatalities, firecracker mutilations, the increased divorced rate, doomsday predictions, inside trading indictments, children falling into abandoned wells, and the firing of our local team's manager. If you question my premise, get a pad and pencil and place it next to your remote control and simply record the various items reported on the news.

We are left frightened and worried. Nothing is nutritionally safe to eat. (And those foods that are safe are fattening or lead to malignancies!) Nowhere is it safe to jog. No one can be trusted.

Why are we seeing all these negatives on our TV screens? Simply because bad news sells. It feasts on our inner fears, and our eyes remain glued. Bad news sells newspapers. It sells magazines. It sells books. We already know we live in a dangerous world and this all serves to confirm the diagnosis.

I would like to propose that in this new century we make a drastic change in the programs that we and our families watch on a regular basis. Just as every TV station is required to allot a certain percentage of time to public service announcements, it should be required (after clearance by First Amendment lawyers) to devote a certain percentage of time to positive, upbeat news. How about 90%! And there is a lot of good stuff going on out there. Good deeds, new inventions, refinements in consumer products, missing children *found*, lost dogs *found*, and animal and bird species, almost extinct, rallying and increasing in number.

Want more? New medications that ease pain and shorten disease, new surgical procedures that miraculously improve hearing or seeing or tasting or something, new fuels that power with less pollution. We need more stories of achievements of the handicapped. We need stories of what amazing unreported good our politicians are doing behind the scenes. Someday, maybe these might be the catchy headlines of our tabloids.

Our sitcoms could be full of compassion, expressions of appreciation, good language and optimism. Like the unwritten rule of the movies of yesteryear in which "crime doesn't pay" in the end, our favorite programs should always climax with the victories going to those on the side of justice.

We all feel better on a mild, breezy, sunny day. We all feel better when we are free of pain and worry, when our loved ones are healthy and prospering. We enjoy fun times. We function best when there is hope and good will and an atmosphere of optimism.

Well, if we want to make this a better world for our grandchildren, let's get a steady diet of this joy into our newspapers and onto our TV screens. Good moods and upbeat attitudes are infectious.

And finally. . . . As we proceed into this new century, our thoughts for improving our lives on this planet should be at the forefront. My grandchildren are counting on it, as are their grandchildren.